HANNAH TREBEC

DOUBLE COVER UP

HANNAH TREBEC

DOUBLE COVER UP

To Stu, & Ngat

Hannah Trebec

Giant Andre Publishing

USA • GERMANY

Hannah Trebec: DOUBLE COVER UP

Copyright © 2012 for the German translation:
Giant Andre Publishing

Copyright © 2012 by Hannah Trebec

All rights reserved. No part of this book may be reproduced or transmitted in any form or by any means, electronic, or mechanical, including photocopying, recording, or by any information storage and retrieval system without written permission from the author and Giant Andre Publishing, except for brief quotations in reviews.

Published in Des Moines, Iowa, by Giant Andre Publishing,
942 Creston Avenue, Suite 202, Des Moines, 50315-1803

First Edition 2012
Printed in the United States of America

ISBN: 978-0-9819847-0-4

Foreword

I want this book dedicated to all law enforcement personnel all over the world. Every country has rules to follow.
I have visited with Hannah Trebec, the author of the book, who was a police officer before the Berlin Wall came down.
We talked about different things; some were different than others. This book will keep you on the edge of your seat how things are done differently. I have been in law enforcement for over 30 years.

    Harold Antle
    Retired Assistant Chief of Police
    Le Grand, Iowa

Acknowledgements

    I would like to thank my immediate family and friends who faithfully stood by my side and encouraged me during the six-year journey of writing this book.

    Special acknowledgement goes to Author Roger Miller and Editor Harold Swihart who coached me with jargon, phrases, and English writing (at times, German differs from other languages.)

    A very appreciative thanks goes to retired Assistant Sheriff Harold Antle for penning the Foreword; Ronald Bauer, Arthur Flatt Sr., Roger Gustafson, and Paula Maxheim for working on the front cover and photography; Marie Soda, Tonya Thoren, and Ryan Wilson for editing assistance; and Anna Rough for her help with American spelling and grammar, especially dialogue.

    I also would like to give special recognition to Marilyn Faidley and Arthur E Flatt Sr. who gave the manuscript the finishing touch.

1

White walls. White closets. White flooring. Even the uniforms were white.

How dull, Manya thought and headed to the counter. Damp brown hair touched the teenager's narrow shoulders. Supported by big brown eyes, her high cheekbones gave her astounding beauty. She unbuttoned her long winter coat, revealing black jeans and a pink knit sweater. The girl hesitated as nurses checked monitors, sorted files, answered phones, scribbled notes, and scurried about amidst flickering lights and ear-numbing buzzers. Stopping close by, a red-haired nurse reviewed a chart.

Manya saw her opportunity and approached. "Excuse me, which room is Michael Mallwitz in?"

The woman in her late fifties looked up. "Are you a relative?"

"I'm his sister."

"Are you eighteen?"

"I'll be sixteen in exactly…" the brunette glanced at the oversized calendar on the wall, "seven weeks and five days."

"We left messages at your parents' work. Do you know when they'll be coming?"

"I don't know about my father but my mother should be here soon."

The nurse pointed to her right. "Your brother is in room one-thirty-five."

"Thank you," the girl said and stepped into the long narrow hallway. Just like the nurses' station, it was laid out in white. Walking briskly, she occasionally checked room numbers.

A rattling noise came from behind. Manya turned around and saw a nurse pushing an empty bed. She stepped aside. Gracefully nodding, the nurse passed.

The girl located her brother's room. As she pushed the door open, a sudden draft swept her hair behind her neck. The weak odor of antiseptic tickled her nose. She studied the room. Two large windows displayed leafless bushes and trees. Beige beds and nightstands and two colorful pictures of children offset the white walls, closets, and flooring.

"Hi, sis!" somebody shouted from the right.

Manya discovered her pre-teen brother in the bed near the windows. He sat up, wearing a white hospital gown. His blond hair was tangled. Dark circles underlined his hazel eyes.

"Michael, there you are!" she happily exclaimed and rushed to his side. The siblings hugged.

"Am I glad to see you. I was starting to feel lonely here," he said, tapping the blanket near his knees.

She sat down and looked around. "Lonely?" The girl pointed at the cluttered nightstand near the door, "What about your roommate?"

"I've never seen him. According to the nurse, he's in surgery."

"You've only been here for a few hours, not days or months…you trouble maker! Mom's worried sick about you."

"You saw Mom?"

"I stopped at the school on the way over here. She told me that she'd come by when she finished tutoring her students and completed the daily activity report." Manya gently stroke his cheek. "Tell me what happened."

"I was playing soccer at recess and tried to bounce the ball off my head. Frank and I jumped up at the same time and collided. When I fell to the ground, I twisted my foot. The ankle swelled up, making my red sock look like a half blown-up balloon. Did you see all the kids crowding around me?"

"I sure did."

He shook his head. "The whispers…the looks…the gestures…. Man, was I embarrassed!"

"I felt for you, especially when the paramedics carried you away on a stretcher. Couldn't they just have given you a pair of crutches?"

"I wish it was that easy. But I also hit my head on the ground, and according to one teacher, passed out."

"I see."

He narrowed his eyes. "Where were you, anyway? I don't recall seeing you."

"Hold on, brother dear," she said, crossing her arms over her chest. "What do you think I was doing? Playing hide-and-seek? I went to the bathroom, for crying out loud! And when I came outside, kids already formed a crowd. One of my classmates told me that you got hurt! I hurried and tried to cut through the crowd, but nobody moved for me."

He sighed. "All right, I believe you."

"May I glimpse at your foot?" she asked, dropping her arms and leaning over.

"Sure," Michael replied and slowly moved his leg. He moaned and curled his hands into fists.

"Are you all right?" Manya inquired.

"I'm okay." He rolled his eyes back. "I should have known better."

"You could just pull the blanket aside."

"Good idea," the boy said, uncovering the lower part of his leg.

She observed his foot. "Oh, my goodness! That looks awful! A half blown-up balloon is an understatement. It looks more like a huge black lump, I'd say."

"It feels like my foot is tied to my leg by a string, kind of like a car tire dangling from a tree limb."

"Really? I bet that's a weird feeling."

"Yep," he replied, nodding. "It sure is."

"I don't see any deformation or bones sticking out. Could it be a sprain? What did the doctors tell you?"

"They've been telling me nothing! However, Frank thinks I tore my ligaments."

"How did he come to that conclusion?"

"His brother experienced something similar last year."

"Even if that was the case, you still would be able to return to soccer in no time, right?"

"Sis, that type of injury is far more complicated than you think. I would actually have to have surgery."

Manya wrinkled her forehead. "Surgery?"

"The ligaments have to be sewn. Otherwise everything could heal incorrectly, greatly limiting my foot's movement and future sports activities."

"Frank told you all that?"

Michael nodded. The girl took off her coat and draped it over the metal frame at the foot end of his bed. "How long was Frank's brother's surgery?"

"I think seven hours."

"Wow, that's almost a third of a day!"

"Manya, I'd rather see the staff take a few extra hours and do a good job, than perform the procedure in five minutes and destroy my, Frank's brother's, or somebody else's future."

"So what's next?"

"The mystery about my condition will be solved once Mom or Dad signs the consent form."

She tapped herself on the forehead. "I understand now. That's why the nurse asked all those questions!"

"You know what the worst part will be?"

"I have no idea."

"The uncomfortable cast."

"That would only be temporary."

"Temporary or not, how am I going to survive this ordeal?" Michael said, looking into his sister's eyes. He gently grabbed her left hand and squeezed it. "How am I supposed to get from point A to point B, dragging a cast like a super-glued bowling ball? Family, friends, school, and soccer; I see a disaster rising. What am I going to do?"

"Listen, brother dear, wearing a cast doesn't mean your life is over. I'm convinced that one of our friends' parents can give you rides from and to school, and we could ask Dad if he is willing to take you to the soccer practices. Doesn't he have afternoon breaks like Mom?"

"I don't know. But why should I go to sports activities when I can't even participate?"

"Are you on a roll today? You're not decapitated or limbless, and you are still part of the team. Go and watch and take as many notes as possible."

"Notes?"

"Yes, notes. You can put them into practice once your cast is off. Just give it a try. That's all I'm asking."

He let go of her hand. "I'll do my best. Do you think Dad will visit today?"

"I'm sure. He'll probably head straight here when he gets off."

"I hope you're right." He watched his sister draw imaginary circles with her right foot. "Thanks for the encouragement."

She hopped off the bed. "Are you thirsty? Have you had anything to drink since recess?"

"I had some tea when I arrived."

"All right, I don't want you to die of thirst in here."

He gazed at Manya and grinned.

"What?" she asked.

"I'm amazed on how much you reflect Mom in caring for others."

"I am her daughter, after all. I just wish you would reflect her more."

"What is that supposed to mean?"

The girl smiled mischievously.

"Oh, sis," Michael said, shaking his head. "You're in big trouble now. Wait until all this is over. I will…" he pushed the blanket aside and kicked his healthy foot into the air. The siblings laughed. "Anyhow," the boy said, scratching his head. "Have you talked to George yet?"

She hopped back on his bed. "I flagged him down after recess and told him that I would get your class material and homework assignments tonight."

"What a relief! I'm so glad you think ahead of things."

The door opened. A man in his fifties entered. The neatly, steam-ironed black suit form-fitted his slender body. Thinning blond hair covered his scalp. His hazel eyes scanned the room as if performing a hospital security check. He focused on the siblings and smiled. "Hello, children!"

The boy and the girl looked up.

"Dad!" Michael shouted with surprise. "You made it!"

Heinrich Mallwitz hugged his son and daughter. "Am I happy to see you!"

The boy observed his father's clothing and wrinkled his forehead. "Why are you wearing this dark suit? The last time I checked, I was still alive."

"I'm sure glad you haven't lost your humor," Heinrich said, patting the boy on the head. "I originally planned on attending my wife's uncle's funeral and family gathering. However, after I got into the office and changed clothes, I found two messages on my desk. One was from your school and the other from the hospital. I called your stepmother to let her know that I'll be late and headed to the hospital. So here I am." He winked at Michael. "Will you be able to keep your foot?"

"Dad, an amputation is out of the question. I probably tore some ligaments. That's it." The boy grinned. "Keep my foot…ha, ha, you're funny."

"Tell me about today's adventure. Spare me no details."

While her brother was talking, Manya quietly left the room. She returned with two wooden chairs and placed them along the side of the bed. Gratefully nodding, her father sat down and stretched his legs.

Manya looked at the empty chair and hopped on the bed. "I hope Mother is coming soon."

Moments later, a middle-aged woman came in. Auburn hair, with a hint of gray, touched the collar of her navy skirt suit. Delicate wrinkles marked the area around her eyes and mouth.

She looked exhausted. Approaching, the woman focused on the boy. "Hello, Michael. How are you, dear? I'm so sorry for not being here sooner, but we were down two teachers today." She hugged the boy, then the girl.

"It's all right, Mom," Michael replied and pointed at the empty chair next to his father. "I'm glad you're here now. Nothing else matters."

The woman looked at her ex-husband. "Hello, Heinrich."

"Hi, Rosemary," the man said, nodding. "It's been a while."

"It's been months," the woman said firmly and sat down. She straightened a few wrinkles on her costume. "I wish you could spend more time with the children. They need you."

"I would spend more time with them if I could. However, I've had too many unexpected things happen, some of which I still have to deal with. Please understand."

Manya loudly cleared her throat. "Mom, Dad, did either one of you sign the consent form and know what's going on with Michael?"

Heinrich shook his head. "I stopped a nurse in the hallway to only get Michael's room number."

"The form is signed," Rosemary said. Looking down, she removed a short white string from the hem of her skirt. "I went to the nurses' station before I came here. Michael's head is fine. However, he tore two ligaments and will need surgery."

"Goodness! Frank was right!" Manya exclaimed and covered her mouth. She gazed at her brother.

"When is my operation?" Michael asked.

"Thursday morning at seven," Rosemary replied.

Michael looked from mother to father. "Will I see you both when I wake up in recovery?"

"I'll see what I can do," Heinrich said.

"I'll be there no matter what," his mother replied. "I already called my boss from the nurses' station, and she agreed to give me the day off."

Manya straightened up and stared at her father. "Dad,

Michael and I would like to ask you something."

"Go ahead."

"We were wondering if you could take Michael to his soccer practices after he gets out of the hospital."

Her father wrinkled his forehead. "Won't he have crutches?"

"Yes, but he's still able to watch and take notes."

"All right. What time is his practice?"

"Five."

Heinrich gave it some thought. "That should work out timewise, since my afternoon break usually starts at a quarter till. However, I work with deadlines and there might be days I won't be available."

"He only practices on Mondays, Wednesdays, and Fridays."

"I'll inform your stepmother; she thinks highly of you two and would be honored to help out."

"But Dad!" Michael exclaimed, wrinkling his forehead. "Are you sure?"

"I'm positive."

"Brother dear," Manya said, "if you feel queasy about it, I'd be happy to go with you."

"I'd like that."

"How is your foot?" Rosemary asked her son.

"It's been better."

His mother rose, walked around the foot end of the bed, and peeked under the blanket. Her eyes widened. "Heinrich, you better take a look at this."

"I pass," her ex-husband said. "Michael's already getting treated, plus I've seen plenty at my construction job."

Rosemary patted her son's arm. "Child, you did a good number on yourself. I've never seen such a swelling and discoloration on anyone's foot. I can only imagine what you must be going through." She kissed the boy on the head.

For the next hour, everybody talked about injuries, operations, school, and life. When nurses wheeled in another bed with an older boy, Heinrich, Rosemary, and Manya departed.

Michael did well during and after surgery. Several days later, he was released from the hospital. After six weeks, he was crutch-free.

2

The hallway lit up. Rosemary quietly entered her daughter's bedroom. She left the door open, shedding some light. Manya lay curled up in her bed, snoring. The woman bent down and gently kissed her daughter's forehead. She whispered, "Good morning, birthday girl."

Manya woke up. "Morning, Mom." Sitting up, the girl stretched her arms and rubbed the sleep out of her eyes.

"Ready for the light?"

Her daughter nodded.

Rosemary activated a nearby switch.

"Oooh," Manya said, temporarily closing her eyes.

Her mother rolled up her cover and placed it at the foot end of the bed. "How do you feel today? Younger, older, wiser?"

The girl shrugged her shoulders. "I feel the same as yesterday, except a little more tired." Lifting her right hand in front of her mouth, Manya stifled a big yawn.

"Tired?" her mother asked. "Were you reading late last night again?"

The girl nodded and smiled. She turned to her nightstand and picked up a burgundy-bound book. "It was so intense, I had to read it till the end."

"That good?"

"Yes!" The teenager, determined, placed the book into her mother's left hand. "It's the best mystery, ever. You've got to read it!"

"I'd love to, but I will be short on time during the next few days."

"I still have a little over two weeks left before it's due back at the library, and I could always extend it! Besides, how long has it been since you've read the last book?"

"All right, you talked me into it." Rosemary tucked the book under her right arm. "Now, back to you, my little bookworm. Are you up to a birthday gathering in the living room?"

"You bet! I've been waiting for that for a year."

A timer buzzed in the kitchen. "I better get the cake out of the oven before it burns," Rosemary said and rushed off.

Manya slipped into a pink bunny-covered fleece robe and pair of matching slippers and followed her mother into the hallway. Walking into the living room, she discovered her brother on the couch. "Hi, Michael."

"Hello, sis," he replied, scrutinizing the girl from head to toe.

"What?" Manya asked. "You've seen me in a robe before…."

"Yes. It's just that I've never seen you in this hopping-bunny set."

"Aunt Brigitta gave the robe and slippers to me last Easter. I forgot all about 'em until I looked for something in my closet last week." Manya spread her arms and rotated three hundred sixty degrees. "What do you think? Do you like what you see?"

"I think for you the set is okay. In regards to me," Michael said and placed his right hand over his heart. "I'm more into boys' stuff and colors, you know."

Flashing eyes, the girl rubbed her face on her raised shoulder. "The robe is really warm and snuggly."

"I pass," Michael said and rolled his eyes back. "Girls!"

After observing the wrapped gifts on the table, Manya checked the floor, looked behind the couch, and circled every chair in the room.

"What's wrong?" her brother asked.

The girl deeply sighed. "I was so hoping for a new bike this year."

"I know how tired you are of riding Mom's squeaky old bicycle. But don't ruin your special day over it! I'm sure the time will come."

Manya's face lit up. "I got it! I'll just cancel my trip this year and stay here to work full-time at a well-paid summer job. I'm sure I'll be able to save enough money by the end of the season."

"What about your friends?" Michael inquired. "They're looking forward to this trip. You really should ask Dad about loaning you some money. He helped me when I needed rides to soccer practices. I'm sure he'd step up for you as well."

"I love your idea and perspective," Manya said, looking under the couch. "But rides are one thing and money another. Do you really think Dad would loan money when Mom's old bike still works? You know what he says: 'if it ain't broke, why replace it?'"

"Manya, you've worked part-time for the past two summers and saved every dime you've made. Dad knows how much you want a bike of your own and how responsible you are…responsible enough that he and Mom even allow you to go on the trip without a parent this year. What reason would Dad have not to loan you the money?"

"Okay, you've got a point," his sister replied, leisurely dropping herself into the closest armchair. "I'll ask him when I see him."

A ceramic dish fell onto the kitchen floor. The children gazed at each other.

"Mom, are you okay in there?" Manya shouted toward the open living room door.

"I'm all right," Rosemary replied.

The children heard their mother sweep up the broken pieces and discard them into the metal garbage can.

Michael looked at his sister, crossed his eyes, and stuck his tongue out. When Manya contorted her face in return, her mother unexpectedly walked in. The girl quickly readjusted her face and gazed at her mother with anticipation.

Rosemary smiled. "I love seeing you two have fun together. It's good for you." She ignited a match and lit a candle. "Michael, would you mind turning the light off, please?"

"Sure," the boy replied, getting up and pulling a switch.

It was still dark out. The dancing flame decorated the walls with funny shadows. Michael and his mother sang two birthday songs. The girl smiled and listened.

Manya blew out the candle and opened her presents. As she thanked her brother and her mother for their gifts, Michael pushed a pink envelope toward her.

"What's this?" she asked, wrinkling her forehead.

Her brother grinned. "A special surprise from everybody."

"Money?"

"Maybe. Maybe not."

Manya anxiously slid her right index finger beneath the flap and tore the envelope open. She discovered a small silver key with engraved numbers. "2611," she read aloud and gazed from brother to mother. "What kind of key is this?"

"If we told you, it wouldn't be a surprise anymore," her mother replied. "Why don't you take a look inside the shed and find out for yourself?"

The girl jumped up and left. Putting their winter coats on, Rosemary and Michael followed her outside. It was unusually warm for December. The ground felt soft.

Manya opened the wooden door. Activating the light switch, she discovered a super-sized cardboard box with her name.

Her mother and her brother caught up and stood at the entrance.

"Is this what I think it is?" Manya asked, eagerly ripping the box into shreds. "Oh-my-goodness…a silver Diamond bike! The best brand that's out there!" The girl happily leaped into the air like an Olympic athlete who'd just won the gold medal.

"Congratulations," her mother said.

"See, your time has come, just like I predicted," Michael said and grinned. He proudly pulled a green bicycle lock from his coat pocket and dangled it in front of his sister's face. Manya grabbed the lock and pinched her brother in the arm.

"Ouch!" Michael screamed. "Mom, she's hurting me!" Rosemary ignored her son and smiled. "Kids."

Manya fastened the lock beneath the saddle. Accompanied by her family, she pushed the bicycle to the front where streetlights illuminated the yard. The wind picked up. Some streetlights flickered. Gently gliding her palm over saddle and frame, the girl inspected her newest gift. "I can't believe this is mine! Oh, Mom! I promise I'll always take care of it. Forever shall it sparkle like an ocean on a sunny day!"

"I had a hard time keeping the secret from you," Michael said.

Manya looked at her mother. "How did you manage such a large purchase on our small budget?"

"Your brother had the brilliant idea to pool money," Rosemary said, patting her son on the shoulder. "He wrote to relatives and visited with numerous friends."

Michael nodded. "I even talked to Dad when he took me to practice one day."

"And?" Manya asked.

"It was mainly his money that helped Mom get the bike."

"Wow…and there I doubted him lending money to me." The girl glanced at the bike and turned to her mother. "Do I have time?"

Rosemary checked her watch. "You've got about eight minutes. I'm sure glad we haven't had any snow yet."

Manya pushed her bike through the narrow picket gate and turned north. She waved at her family and hopped on. With every pedal stroke, the girl gently bounced her body off the saddle as if riding a horse. Manya continuously smiled.

After going up and down the street several times, the girl returned. Rosemary patted her daughter on the back. "You reminded me of a toddler on a sugar-high."

"Toddler? Sugar-high?" Thrusting her fists up, Manya shouted, "I'm happy!"

"Good, now let's eat breakfast."

The girl put her bike away and joined her family inside. After breakfast, Manya hugged her brother and her mother at the table. "Thanks for your help in getting me the best present ever!"

3

Somebody rang the bell and knocked on the door. Michael answered. A girl with thick waist-length blond hair stood outside, breathing heavily. She looked a few years older than the boy. Her face was wet. Sweat drenched her light blue dress on her chest and under the arms.

Michael scratched his head. "Anke, what are you doing here? Are you okay?"

"I'm…all right," the girl said and stepped inside.

Michael closed the door and shouted toward the end of the hallway. "Manya, Anke is here!"

His sister came out of her room. "Anke? What's going on?"

"I know it's past nine, and I apologize," her best friend said. "But I just couldn't wait until tomorrow."

Manya reached for Anke's right hand and pulled her into the living room. She closed the door. "Couldn't wait with what?"

"Very exciting news!"

"Are you inheriting a million marks from some rich West German uncle?"

Anke shook her head. "Something way better: I'm getting married!"

"You're what?"

"I'm getting married!" Anke said, joyfully jumping up and down. "Heiko proposed to me this evening, and I accepted."

"Wow! I'm so happy for you! I knew you two were going out tonight, but I never suspected this kind of turnout."

"I didn't either. I'm so excited!" The girls ecstatically danced around the table and chairs while singing old-fashioned love songs.

Rosemary entered. "What's going on in here? I could hear your commotion down in the basement."

"Heiko proposed to Anke today," Manya said. "Can you believe that?"

Her mother looked at the future bride. "Well, congratulations, young lady. What a pleasant surprise. I wish you two the very best and hope to be invited."

"Of course you'll be invited," Anke said.

Michael walked in. "What did I hear? Anke got engaged? Does Heiko know what he's getting into?"

"Get out of here!" Manya shouted. She picked up a couch pillow and threw it at her brother. Michael ducked. The pillow missed his head by a few centimeters and landed in the corridor.

The boy stuck his tongue out and wiggled his body. "You can't hit me, ha, ha."

Rosemary picked up the pillow and tapped her son on the rear with it. "But I can hit you right there, and not only with a pillow. Teasing your sister and her best friend? Seems like I'll have to teach you some better manners." Rosemary tossed the pillow onto the couch and …smiled. "What can I say: children."

"I get the hint," Michael said and winked at Anke. "If it doesn't work out, you can always marry me."

Rosemary put her right arm around her son and walked him out.

Manya waited until she heard two doors close in the hallway. "So tell me, how did he propose?"

"After Heiko and I had dinner, the waiter placed two small heart-shaped chocolate cakes on the table. My dessert had a white round cardboard box on top. Puzzled, I gazed at Heiko. He nodded and said, 'Go ahead and open it.' I removed the lid and almost passed out when I saw the engagement ring. Heiko smiled, got on his knees, and asked me to marry him."

"How romantic! Did you bring that precious token of love?"

"Naturally," Anke said. Pulling her hair over the right shoulder to the front, she revealed a gold necklace. "I love my hair…besides braiding and styling, it also comes in handy at times." The girl carefully rotated the necklace. A locket appeared.

"Did Heiko give you that too?" Manya asked, taking a

closer peek. "I've never seen it before."

"No, that's an heirloom from my grandmother. This is the first and the last time that I will wear it. Gold. Too valuable, you know. I think my mom would flip if she saw it on me." Anke opened the locket. She removed an engagement band and handed it over. "Take a look."

Manya inspected the ring from various angles. "Gorgeous, absolutely gorgeous! I know it's gold. But what is that clear stone in the center?"

"According to Heiko, it's a diamond."

"A diamond…how classy! Why aren't you wearing it?"

"Because I wanted you to see it first."

Manya hugged her friend. "Oh, Anke! I feel so special. You are like the sister I never had."

"Same goes for you. What would I do without you, especially after all these years? With my brothers always picking on me, I think I probably would have gone insane by now."

"Can't be that bad," Manya said and watched her friend put the ring on her finger.

Gazing at her hand, Anke tilted her head to the right and tilted her head to the left. "I guess I'll keep it!"

"The ring suits you well."

"Thank you."

"Did you guys set a date yet?"

"December second of next year, right after I turn eighteen."

"What did his parents say?" Manya inquired. "Do you know?"

"Heiko said that they didn't expect a proposal so soon but were very happy for us. They even revealed a secret."

"What kind of secret?"

"When Heiko marries, he'll inherit his grandfather's house and part of the estate."

"Wow, you'll have money, a house, and a loving husband. What a fairy tale!"

"Heiko certainly is a prince." Anke paused and sighed. "I

hope some day you'll be as lucky."

"As long as I meet him after graduation from language school. I'd like to secure a good job and some money first."

"Wise thinking."

Manya eyed her friend from neck to toe. "I can definitely picture you in a fluffy white dress."

"Fluffy and with lots of lace, please. Would you like to be the maid of honor and pick out a dress with me?"

"I'd be delighted to," Manya said. "However, don't forget that once I start language school, I'll only be home on weekends."

"We still have time until then." Anke dropped the locket under her dress and pulled her hair to the back. Thunder roared from a distance. The girl widened her eyes and stared at Manya. "I better head back home before the storm gets much closer," she said. "If I get hit by lightning, the wedding will never take place!"

Grinning, Manya patted her friend on the shoulder. "If you get hit by lightning, I don't think you'll have to worry about anything anymore." She walked her friend out.

Ear-numbing thunder vibrated the ground. The girls quickly hugged.

Anke hustled down the steps and got on her bicycle. Shouting, "I'll see you tomorrow!" she sped off.

4

Manya stepped into the living room. Bright sun shone through the half-closed yellow drapes and highlighted the green area rug near the windows. The girl glanced over the brown leather furniture before resting her eyes on her mother. Rosemary sat on the couch, knitting. Manya cleared her throat. "Mom, do you have a moment?"

Her mother stopped knitting and looked up. "I sure do." She placed the needles on top of the yarn in her lap and patted the couch area beside her. "Have a seat. What would you like to talk about?"

"Michael and I have noticed that you've been very reserved for the past few days. You don't joke, don't smile, or have long conversations with either one of us. You're not sick, are you?"

"No, I'm fine."

"Did either one of us do something you disapproved of?"

"No, not at all."

"I know something is on your mind! You strive for family values, unity, and harmony, and you always encourage Michael and me to communicate when we have a problem. I think it's your turn. Please tell me what's been bothering you. Does it have anything to do with the trip tomorrow?"

Rosemary put her arm around her daughter and looked into her eyes. "All right, I'll tell you what's on my mind. I'm extremely uncomfortable with you children going on this bike ride without adult supervision."

"But Mother, we already discussed this last week! You agreed that I could go. You even said that I've matured over the last couple of years. What brought up the change?"

Rosemary tenderly pushed a hair strand from her daughter's face. "A friend from work and I had a long discussion."

"You're not calling it off, are you?"

The doorbell rang. "I'll get it," Manya said and rose. A tear rolled down her cheek. Rosemary followed her daughter into the hallway. The girl wiped her face with her hand and opened the door. "Dad!"

"Hello, pumpkin!" Heinrich greeted and kissed his daughter on the cheek.

"I'm so delighted to see you!" Manya exclaimed, hugging her father. "What a surprise! Please come in."

Heinrich stepped inside and saw his ex-wife in the corridor. "Good evening, Rosemary."

"Hello, Heinrich."

"What brings you here today?" Manya asked.

"I came to wish my big daughter farewell before she leaves for the first unsupervised trip of her life."

"Oh, Daddy," Manya said sadly and shook her head. "If you only knew!"

"Know what?" her father inquired and turned to Rosemary. "What's going on?"

"Do you remember Ursula Bauer from work?"

"I do," Heinrich replied, wrinkling his forehead. "What does she have to do with anything?"

"Well, Ursula told me that she had a bad feeling about Manya going without an adult this year. I now have second thoughts."

"Rosemary, don't revoke or base decisions on other people's instincts! I believe Manya is capable of handling situations better than you think. She is cautious, reliable, and smart. In a couple of years, the girl will be an adult and could even get married if she wanted to. For crying out loud, our daughter deserves a little independence! Let her grow up! Besides, do you realize how much this trip means to her?"

"All right," Rosemary replied. "Since you're convinced that Manya is competent enough, I'll let her go."

"Thank you, Mom! Thank you, Dad! Yoo-hoo!" Manya cheered and clapped her hands.

Rosemary placed a hand on her daughter's shoulder. "However, you'll need to promise me a couple of things."

"I'll do anything."

"First: I would like you to always stick together as a group when you travel."

"Sure, we can do that."

"And second: as soon as you arrive in Mark's town, I'd like you to send me an urgent telegram."

"Consider it done."

Focusing on his daughter, Heinrich pointed his right index finger at her. "Remember your mother's words. We love you too much to have something happen to you."

"Yes, Father, I understand."

"I'll better leave you two alone," Rosemary said and disappeared into the living room.

Manya and her father went into the kitchen. "Where's your brother tonight?" Heinrich asked, joining his daughter at the table. "He usually would have clung to me like a monkey by now."

"Michael is at a friend's birthday party. He should be back within a couple of hours or so."

"I see."

"Guess what happened to Anke last week," Manya said cheerfully.

"She found a hundred-mark bill?"

"No, something much better: Heiko proposed to her."

"He did?" Heinrich rubbed his chin. "In a way it doesn't really surprise me. Haven't those two love birds been going out since they were thirteen?"

"Yes, and everybody thought it was puppy love. Just look at 'em now. Their bonds are stronger than ever."

Her father uttered. "Never underestimate the power of love." He leaned over and patted his daughter's left hand. "Pumpkin, one of these days you'll fall in love too, and I so much dread the thought of giving you away."

"Oh, Daddy, quit it! You're bringing tears to my eyes."

"All right," he said and leaned back. "Please congratulate Heiko and Anke for me, and tell 'em that I wish the very best for their future."

"I will." Repeatedly gliding her finger over a stitched flower on the tablecloth, Manya lowered her head.

"What's the matter?"

Without taking her eyes off the table, she replied, "Dad, Michael and I really appreciated the rides to the soccer practices. However, it seems that ever since Michael's cast went bye-bye, you were gone as well. Did Michael or I do something wrong?"

Her father shook his head. "No, neither one of you did anything wrong."

"So what is it? You're not getting divorced, are you?"

"No, absolutely not!"

"Can you talk about it?" She lowered her voice. "I promise I won't tell anyone, not even Michael."

Rosemary turned the television on. Leaning over, Manya's father gently pushed the door shut. He deeply inhaled. "During the past couple of years, your stepmother and I encountered numerous difficulties. Elizabeth's two miscarriages by far hit us the most since we so desperately wanted children." Manya reached for her father's hand. He slowly continued. "The losses put my wife in month-long depressions. We gave up on having children. However, a few months before your brother got hurt, Elizabeth became pregnant again. She was plagued by nausea, vomiting, colds, running temperatures, swollen feet, and gestational diabetes."

Manya wrinkled her forehead. "Your wife seemed okay when she gave Michael and me the two rides to Michael's practice."

"That was the beginning of the second trimester which had the least occurrences."

"Was she able to carry the baby full term?"

"Yes, she was. But now, I hardly get to see my wife or child." He shook his head. "I feel like my life is jinxed."

"How come you hardly see 'em?"

"I was promoted to a job with mandatory overtime."

"You should have told us what was going on. We would

have understood."

"Michael's incident, your birthday, finals, the upcoming trip…I figured you already had enough to handle."

"Dad, family comes first," Manya said. "If I only had known…I feel bad for judging you."

"It's all right," he said, checking his watch. Heinrich rose and hugged his daughter. "It's getting late. You need your rest to fuel up for the trip tomorrow."

"Wait!" The girl grasped his arm. "How are your wife and child now?"

"Elizabeth has fully recovered, and the baby is fine."

"What's the baby's name?"

"Amelia."

"A-me-li-a," Manya slowly repeated. "What a cute name! I like her already. Could I meet her sometime?"

"I'll try to put something together upon your return. Maybe we can have a picnic or so."

"Sounds like a plan."

He wrote something on a piece of paper and gave it to her. "My family and I moved yesterday. This is my current address. I'd like you to send me a telegram as well."

"Okay."

"Oh, before I forget…" Heinrich opened his wallet and removed a hundred-mark bill. "This should cover all telegram costs and give you some extra. Have a pizza party on me or do whatever you like."

"Wow! Thanks, Dad," Manya said and followed her father outside.

Heinrich hugged his daughter. "Love you. Have a great trip. My thoughts will be with you."

"Bye, Dad. Love you too." As she watched her father take off, her eyes filled with tears.

5

The scent of fried bacon, eggs, and potatoes greeted Manya in the hallway. She wore a pink cotton pantsuit. Her hair was combed. Checking the wall-mounted wardrobe rack, the girl located no additional jackets. The space under the waist-high storage closet also only revealed the same pairs of shoes from the night before. Mmmh, no unexpected guests, Manya thought and walked into the kitchen. Shielded by a red full-sized apron, her mother stood at the stove and stirred the ingredients in their largest frying pan.

"Morning, Mom," the girl said. "What are you doing here? Are we expecting anybody?"

Rosemary momentarily looked up. "Surprise!" Turning the knob clockwise, she reduced the flames to a minimum. "I took a couple of hours off to fix something special and have breakfast with Michael and you. Have a seat. It'll be ready in a few minutes."

Manya sat down and glanced at the steaming frying pan. Her stomach growled. "The farmer's breakfast looks and smells so delicious," the girl said. "The scent is clear out in the hallway. Since Michael loves food and leaves his door open at night, I'm surprised he isn't waiting at the table with the fork in his hands." Rosemary smiled. Manya scratched her right cheek. "I wonder why people call it farmer's breakfast?"

"Probably because that's what German farmers used to and might still eat before heading to the field. Potatoes have starch, and starch gives you energy. The name most likely evolved over time. I think German farmers and their potatoes are inseparable like tar and feathers."

"Oooh, Mom," Manya said. "Tar and feathers sound really gross at the table; I'm not sure if I'm as hungry anymore." Her mother turned the stove off, picked up the skillet, and approached. She evenly scooped the food onto three plates.

Narrowing her eyes, Rosemary raised her wooden spoon.

"Not as hungry anymore, huh? Just like a farmer you should strengthen yourself before heading out into the …wild. Your cycling will take a lot of energy. Besides, I made efforts to spoil you children this morning." Her mother placed spoon and frying pan into the nearby sink. "So you better eat up."

"I wouldn't mind having this type of breakfast every day."

"Now, don't you get carried away, young lady!" Smiling, Rosemary shook her head. "Go and check on your brother."

Grinning, the girl rose. Michael came into the kitchen and wordlessly sat at the table. All colors had faded from his face. His hair stood up. The top button of his striped pajamas hung by a thread. Looking down, he stared at his plate.

"Are you okay?" Manya inquired and slowly sat down. "What's going on?"

Without taking his eyes of the food, Michael shook his head.

"Let's eat while the food is still warm," Rosemary said.

After the meal, the children's mother cleaned the table and left the kitchen. The entrance door shut.

"Can you tell me now?" Manya asked her brother.

Michael rubbed his eyes and deeply exhaled. "I woke up from a horrifying dream last night and was unable to go back to sleep for several hours."

"You had a nightmare? About what?"

"You."

"Me?" Manya said, stunned. "You rarely ever have dreams, and out of the blue, you dream about me?"

"Yes, I'm telling you the truth."

"How bad was it?"

"You don't wanna know," Michael said.

"Tell me!"

Making a grim face, her brother shouted, "I stood in a dark room looking at a coffin, okay!"

"A coffin?"

"Yes, and that's all I'm gonna tell you," he calmly said.

Manya wrinkled her forehead and stared at the loose button on her brother's pajamas.

Moving his chair closer, he reached for his sister's right hand and looked deep into her eyes. "Please don't go! I'm so scared something might happen to you."

"Michael, don't do this to me," the girl said and retreated. "Stop worrying! I'll be fine. I promise I'll use extra caution and good judgment in everything I do, okay? Besides, Heiko and Anke will be with me as well. What could possibly happen?"

He held his left small finger toward his sister. "Pinky promise that you'll always be careful?"

"Pinky promise," she assured, hooking both small fingers into his finger. "Thanks for the concern, and I'm sorry about your bad dream."

"Thank goodness I don't dream every night."

Staring at the clock above the door, Manya rose. "I better get going…still need to pack lunch, take my bags outside, get the bike from the shed, and strap the luggage on."

"I'll help you."

Manya checked the counter. Except for a small bottle of apple juice, it was empty.

Rosemary peeked in. "If you're looking for the sandwiches, they're already on the bike."

"You strapped them to the bike?" Manya asked.

"Of course not…join me outside!"

Without paying attention to the hallway, the children followed Rosemary to the front yard. Manya's bicycle leaned against the fence near the gate. With the help of a bungee cord, the rear rack held the girl's large red duffel bag. A black backpack sat on top.

"Wow! Mom, you were busy this morning," Manya said, picking up her backpack and pulling its straps over her shoulders. "I thought everything was still in the corridor."

"That's what mothers are for," Rosemary said and kissed her daughter on the cheek. "I love you." She tapped on her watch.

"Child, you need to keep moving!"

Manya quickly hugged her brother and her mother and got on her bicycle. Michael held the gate open. "I will miss you."

"Likewise," the girl said and, after checking for traffic, walked her bicycle into the street. She smiled, waved, and took off.

"Remember the telegrams!" her mother shouted.

"I will!"

Moments later, Manya turned into a side street and disappeared.

6

One foot on the ground, one foot on the pedal, Anke sat on her bike and waited. Over the rear tire, a mounted steel basket held two blue bags that surpassed the height of the saddle by several inches. The combined excessive weight made the tires look half deflated.

Anke looked at the lower portion of her green knit top and pulled it out of her jeans. Tying her hair into a ponytail, she gazed at Heiko. Her fiancé, tall and slender, stood between her and the chain-link fence of her residence. His thighs held his bike in place. She compared the luggage. Equipped with only one bag, Anke wondered why he always seemed to have less. His red hair drew her attention. Short and spiked, it reminded her of a hedgehog. She grinned.

"Thanks for wearing the khaki outfit I bought you last week," Anke said. "It goes well with your freckles."

Preoccupied, he stared at the west end of the street and checked his watch. "Two minutes late. I'll give her a few more moments."

"Two minutes late?" Anke shook her head. "Thank goodness, she doesn't live further away! Your desire for punctuality annoys me, especially since we're on summer break and have all the time in the world. Maybe something came up. What if her basement got flooded by the heavy rain from last night?" The couple exchanged looks.

"Maybe she changed her mind," Heiko said.

Anke rolled her eyes. "Get real!"

Brake-pressured tires dug into nearby soil.

"I hope you two were not arguing about me," a female voice asked. The couple turned heads.

"Manya!" Anke exclaimed. "Am I glad you're here! Heiko is driving me crazy."

"Not as crazy as my past twenty-four hours have been. I

almost stayed home."

"What happened?" Heiko asked.

The girl told her friends about her mother's sudden objection to the trip, her father's unexpected visit and rescue, and Michael's eerie nightmare.

"Honestly," Anke said, tightening her ponytail, "if I were your brother and had the same dream, I would've asked you to stay home on my knees. One of my brothers, on the other hand, would have most likely deflated my tires."

"Thanks, but no thanks," Manya said. "Now I really have second thoughts."

Speechless, Anke stared at her fiancé.

Heiko shrugged his shoulders. "Don't look at me, girl. It's up to her. I won't twist her arm to make her do anything. But if she goes, I personally guarantee that she'll be safe with us. I'd guard her like a lump of gold during the California Gold Rush."

"Manya, please," Anke said. "I'll go on my knees, or do whatever it takes…besides, you know Heiko is a man of his word, and who knows when you actually will have time for a next trip."

Giving it some thought, Manya said, "All right, I'll go."

"Thank you, Manya!" Anke happily shouted and clapped her hands. She embraced her friend. "Thank you so much! You're a wonderful person. I have a feeling that this is going to be a trip we will always remember."

"Before I forget…" Manya said, recalling her mother's last words. "Once we are in town, I do need to stop at the post office."

"For what?" Anke asked.

"I promised my parents a telegram upon arrival."

"What a brilliant idea! I should send one to my mother as well."

"I wouldn't do that if I were you."

"Why?"

"Your mom doesn't expect it and might think that something happened."

"I don't want that," Anke said and crossed looks with her

fiancé.

"I have an idea," Manya said. "I'll just add a note to my mother's telegram, asking her to stop at your house."

"Excellent!"

"Are you ladies ready to follow?" Heiko inquired.

The girls nodded. After checking for traffic, the small convoy took off.

Two hours passed. Heiko unexpectedly slowed down and fell back. "I need to take a break. I last ate several hours ago and am getting really hungry. My stomach is growling like an angry wolf."

Turning her head sideways, Anke shouted, "My goodness, you and your fast metabolism! I can see it already: when we're old and gray and on social security, you'll eat the hair off my head. I didn't know it before, but I do now: the only reason you picked me was because of my thick hair!" Everybody chuckled.

Manya pointed at an upcoming grassy area with a large shady oak and a forest in the background. "Let's stop there!"

They pulled off the road, followed a narrow trail, leaned their bikes against the tree, and sat in the shade. Manya looked up. "I wonder how old this oak is?"

Anke and Heiko inspected the wide trunk and crown. A sparrow flew out.

"Judging by its size, very old," Anke said and gazed at the street. "Did you two notice that not one car has passed since we got here?" She sighed. "It's so peaceful."

"And, compared to yesterday, we have a cloudless sky," Heiko said.

Manya bit into her sandwich. The wind carried a strange scent from the forest.

"Whoa!" Anke shouted. She stared at the unwrapped sandwich in her lap, as if it came from another planet. Holding her nose shut, Manya, amused, gazed at Anke.

"Coming to think of it…about a month ago, I heard about a new stable," Heiko said. "It was supposed to be somewhere around here." He tilted his head toward the forest. "I bet it's behind those trees."

"If you two want to trespass, go ahead," Manya said. "I'm fine right here. My mother taught me better manners."

Realigning salami slices without the former overlap, Heiko cleared his throat. "Actually, I think the forest is public property."

"Are you sure?" Manya asked.

"Pretty much. At least, it used to be according to my now-deceased grandfather."

Anke's eyes lit up. "Do we have enough time to check it out?"

"Certainly," Heiko replied and bit into his sandwich. "For you…anything."

"Remember that we still need to go to the post office," Manya said.

"We gonna be okay," he assured and concentrated on his sandwich.

After the picnic, the teenagers followed the trail through the forest. Hill up, hill down; curve left, curve right; passing oaks, maples, firs, and spruces; riding, falling and rising on their bicycles, the group arrived at a clearing.

A wooden fence stretched from east to west for several hundred meters. Inside, black, white, brown, gray; tall and short horses trotted or galloped everywhere. Mud covered the trampled, withering grass. Small enclosed birch trees were gnawed to limbless stubs.

Anke closed her eyes. "I'm in paradise."

Manya placed her right palm on the forehead. "Paradise? Just look at those young trees inside the fence."

"Anke, your love for horses is astounding," Heiko said. "I hope you love me just as much." He rolled his eyes. "You're such a fanatic."

Manya pointed at a small horse on the left. "Do you see that black colt? He just rammed his head into another horse. Does he think he's a bull?"

Anke laughed. "He sure is cute. I wish I could pat him." She gently dropped her bicycle and approached the fence.

"Don't get too close," Heiko said and followed his fiancée.

Snorting, the colt galloped to a close black mare and lowered his head. The mare nipped him on the back and … nursed him.

"I can't pass this up," Manya said loudly. She leaned her bike on a nearby tree and retrieved her camera from her backpack. After taking several shots from the clearing, she approached the couple. "How about a few pictures of you two while I'm at it?"

"Sure," Anke replied, untying her ponytail and spreading her hair over her shoulders. She reached for her fiancé's arm and pulled him closer. "Just make sure the colt is in the background of at least a few of 'em."

Manya took picture after picture.

"I think that's enough," Heiko said and bowed once to his future wife and once to Manya. "May I have the honor and take some snapshots of you ladies now?"

"Absolutely!" Anke replied. "You're such a gentleman."

Manya handed the camera to Heiko and joined her friend near the fence. "You two are indisputably made for each other."

"Give me the biggest smile you've got!" Heiko said.

The girls posed like models: sitting, standing, hugging, or leaning back-to-back against each other.

"Yes! Beautiful! Just like that!" he cheered. "I love how that light breeze plays with your hair! How about adding some creativity?"

Anke put one arm around Manya and held the other one up as if catching invisible raindrops. "Like this?"

"Yes! Perfect! How about you girls holding hands in front of the old oak?"

"Excellent idea," Manya said.

"Can we stop here on our way home?" Anke asked.

"I don't see why we couldn't," Heiko replied.

They returned to the oak tree. Heiko continued his photo shoot until he ran out of film.

Stowing the camera, Manya said, "I can't wait to hang these pictures in my dorm."

"We couldn't have asked for a better pit stop," Anke noted and hugged Manya. "Thank you."

Gazing at his watch, Heiko wrinkled his forehead. "What? Three already? I didn't realize how fast the time has gone by. We better get going. Who knows how long the lines will be at the post office."

An hour later, the group arrived at the yellow city sign. Heiko signaled the girls to stop. "Do either one of you know where the Halle Post Office is?" he asked.

Anke and Manya looked at each other and shook their heads.

Heiko flagged down an older man on a bike. After a short conversation, he returned. "It's at the opposite edge of town." The teenagers rushed off.

Thirty minutes later, they pushed their bikes into the bicycle rack at the post office.

"I've…got to…take…a break," Anke said, heavily breathing. She sat on the concrete bench in front of the building and stretched her legs. Heiko joined and slowly rubbed her back.

"Are you okay?" Manya asked.

Her friend nodded.

"Go ahead," Heiko said and pointed at the entrance. "Don't wait for us."

The girl went inside. When she returned, Anke was by herself. Looking around, Manya asked, "Where's Heiko?"

Anke pointed at the bakery across the street. "He's getting us some treats."

"Oh."

Heiko came out of the store, carrying a white paper sack. He crossed the street and approached. "Were you ladies talking about me?"

"Maybe," Anke replied.

"You two better behave, or I'll devour all desserts by myself."

"I don't think so," his fiancée said, reaching for the bag. He flirtatiously pulled it away.

"Hey!" Anke yelled and protruded her lower lip like a sulking toddler.

Heiko gave her the paper sack. "Okay, you may have a piece since you did such a great job pedaling and pouting."

She looked inside. "Wow, tummy yummies: cherry-filled pastries and cheesecake squares. You're the best!"

They ate and headed to Mark's place.

7

The teenagers stopped at a white two-story home with a black picket fence. Yellow rose bushes aligned the path to the house. The lawn was neatly trimmed. Heiko and the girls put the bikes in the back and came up front. Manya quickly smelled a rose before joining the couple at the top of the steps. Anke rang the bell.

A man in his twenties opened the door. Wavy black hair cast no doubt of the Basque ancestry he had mentioned to Manya in his last letter. Massive muscles tightened the short sleeves of his white top. His clean-shaved face, wide chest, and form-fitted jeans made him very appealing.

"Hi, I'm so happy to see you guys!" Mark exclaimed. "The past year seemed like a century. C'mon in."

The people hugged in the hallway.

"A century, huh?" Anke said. "That would make you … very old. I'm surprised you even remembered us." She glanced at the narrow brown coat rack, green wardrobe closet, and orange wallpaper near Mark's head. "The house still looks the same though." Anke looked up. "Except for those spider webs."

"Here, let me get the broom for you," Mark said and opened the closet.

She raised her hands toward him. "No, no, it's okay."

"Just kidding." Retrieving two red roses and two large chocolate bars from the closet, he said, "I do have some gifts for you and Manya."

"Chocolates and roses?" Anke joyfully accepted one of each. "Your welcome presents are getting better by the year! What will they be next? Cars?"

The man laughed and turned to Manya. "And a rose and a chocolate for you, my dear friend."

"Thank you," the girl said, turning red.

Heiko watched his fiancée devour all of her chocolate.

"Mark, you're spoiling the girls way too much. One of these days it might go to their heads."

"Whether you realize it or not, every woman needs attention." Mark turned and unhooked a stuffed burgundy bag from the coat rack. "But I've got a surprise for you as well."

"A gift for me? What's gotten into you? We still have a few months until Christmas."

"I should have thought about this a long time ago, but better late than never."

Heiko opened the bag and removed a white plastic box with a large red cross on top. "A First-Aid kit! I could always use one of these. Thank you, man!"

"Mark is such a nice person," Anke said. "Don't you agree, Manya?" The girl nodded and caressed the petals on her rose.

"Let's look at reality," Mark said. "I missed our rummy games, pizza parties, and long conversations and better be kissing up! Otherwise, I could become a pretty lonely man without you guys."

"Still working that odd three-shift factory job of yours?" Heiko asked.

"Yep."

"If I were you, I would have found something else a long time ago."

"Heiko, jobs are limited around here, especially the ones that pay well."

"Don't the hours and monotonous work wear you out?"

"They do," Mark said. "But a job is a job and when you guys come, I take my vacation and relax."

Heiko shook his head. "Vacation at home? You're crazy! If I had time and money, I'd want to see the world."

"Honestly, I'd rather be here," Mark said, pointing at the walls around him. "I'm a home buddy."

"My grandfather always said, 'home is were most people die.'"

"I've heard of that. But the statement doesn't scare me.

As long as you guys visit every year, I'd at least die happy." He pointed at a door at the end of the hallway. "What are you guys standing around here for? Go and sprawl in the living room! You've got to be tired. I'll be in shortly with refreshments."

Manya, Anke, and Heiko went into the living room. They froze near the door and stared. Mark had new furniture. A cushioned green sofa stood where the beat-up daybed used to be. Majestic armchairs surrounded a rectangular table with carved legs, replacing the old mismatched barstools and two round tables.

"Wow!" Manya shouted. "I love this!"

"Look," Anke said, pointing at a large picture above the couch. "Mountains with trees."

Manya plopped herself crosswise on the closest armchair. Her feet dangled over the armrest. "This is so comfy." She repositioned her head and observed the new picture.

"Let's try the couch," Anke said.

Heiko widened his eyes. "Honey!"

"Not that way!" the girl said, rolling her eyes. She pulled her fiancé to the couch and sprawled next to him.

Mark came in. He set four cups and plates; a platter with meatballs speared by toothpicks, and a ceramic jug on the table.

"Excellent job with the decorating, Mark," Manya said.

"I thought it was time, plus I know how green reminds you of nature. I want you and the others to feel comfortable around here."

"Well, I think you succeeded. Although, you could have replaced the orange wallpaper."

"Well, I could take the dishes back out, and you can get the meatballs and lemonade yourself from the kitchen," Mark said, reaching for the platter.

Manya gently pushed his hand away. "Everything's fine right here."

"Women…" He smirked at Heiko. Carefully pouring Anke's drink, Mark said, "Back to reality, Manya mentioned in her last letter that you and Heiko have some unexpected news."

"Yes, Heiko and I are getting married."

"You're what?" Lowering the jug, he spilled some lemonade.

"We're getting married," she said, kissing her fiancé on the cheek. "Heiko proposed to me and I accepted."

"Huh, I had no idea. Congratulations!" He filled the rest of the cups and sat across from Manya. "Tell me more."

Taking turns, Heiko and Anke talked about the proposal at the restaurant, their parents' reactions, the inheritance, and the current wedding plans.

Mark, satisfied, nodded and said, "Wow, you two will already have a house to move into and some pocket change. What more could newlyweds possibly ask for?"

"All these years…and my parents never mentioned anything," Heiko said.

"I would have done the same. Be honest. If you had known, would you have worked as hard on your grades, done those summer jobs, and selected the same apprenticeship?"

"Probably not. I see where they're coming from," he said, picking up a meatball. He leisurely placed it on his tongue, closed his mouth, and pulled out the toothpick.

"To the planned wedding…" Mark said, scratching his scalp. "You mentioned you wanted me to be the best man? I'm not sure if I want that job since it comes with a challenge."

Wrinkling her forehead, Anke stared at him. "What are you talking about?"

"Don't you know that the best man keeps the maid of honor under control? Manya is heavy duty and represents an overwhelming challenge."

"Under control? Overwhelming challenge?" Standing up, Anke crossed her arms over her chest and tilted her head. "Like that really applies to Manya! She wouldn't even crush a bug if her life depended on it. I think you've taken way too many liberties. First you shower us with gifts, then you wanted to deprive us of food, and now you pick on us? If I were you, I wouldn't look too far, Mr. Innocent. I wonder who really needs to be controlled here?" Raising her right hand, the girl slapped the air, and … grinned. She sat down.

Heiko patted his fiancée on the back. "I love your humor. You sure had me going for a while. I thought we'd end up in a fistfight. I swear you were born a comedian." He turned to Manya who had just stuffed a meatball into her mouth. "Girl, you better be careful around Mark. You know the saying: those who tease each other love each other. Although, we could always have a double wedding."

Manya stopped chewing.

Mark cleared his throat. "Funny stuff aside. I admire Manya. She's a very remarkable and wise young woman… wise especially, by putting academics before other interests. She worked hard to get her good grades. A serious relationship, for example with a guy like me, could not only endanger her future but also destroy it. Manya wants to go to language school. So be it. She'll always have my support, no matter what. I believe that the sacrifices we make today will help us reach the stars tomorrow."

"Thank you, Mark," Manya said. "I'm flattered by the way you think about me. A good friend like you is hard to come by."

Heiko squeezed his fiancée's hand and looked at Manya. "Anke and I support your decisions as well and will always be there for you."

"I love you guys," Manya said and finished her lemonade. "Let's stay friends forever."

Anke held her right hand over the table. "Forever it shall be." Her fiancé, Mark, and Manya slapped their hands on top. The pile disbanded.

Picking up the last meatball, Mark asked, "Shall we have an engagement party tomorrow night?"

"Yes!" Anke shouted and cheerfully clapped.

"Definitely," Manya said. "I could order cake from the

bakery. My dad was very generous this year."

Mark nodded. "You order cake, and I'll get the rest."

"Consider it done."

"I'm so looking forward to tomorrow," Anke said, tugging on her fiancé's upper arm. Heiko smiled. The group happily chatted for several hours.

At midnight, only Mark and Manya remained, discussing politics, freedom, and the Berlin Wall.

8

Wearing pink silk pajamas, Anke entered the kitchen. Her hair was tangled. I wonder if Mark changed anything in here, she thought and checked her surroundings. The oversized beige cupboards and countertop hadn't been replaced. Even the old manual breadslicer and steel immersion heater were still there, waiting for the next job. A muffled fan hummed near the window. She turned around. I almost forgot…the Russian fridge. What, twenty years Mark said last summer? Those things seem to last forever.

Yawning, she covered her mouth with her right hand and peeked at the clock above the door. What? Nine fifteen already? Where is everybody? Anke set the table, filled the immersion heater with water, and plugged it in. Leaning her back against the counter, she focused on the glass vase on the table. Both roses had opened. Manya will be so excited when she sees that.

Thinking about the 'Friends-for-ever' pact from yesterday, she sighed. I so wish that Mark and Manya could become a couple. As she daydreamed about the Plaenterwald amusement park in Berlin, her feet tingled. Interlocking arms with Manya, she could see herself and her best friend stroll hand-in-hand with Heiko and Mark from attraction to attraction. Laughing or screaming, the four of them would bounce or twirl on rides, high up in the sky.

Large bubbles percolated in the immersion heater, pulling Anke back to reality. She unplugged the device and made tea.

Holding the teapot, Anke moved the vase to make room. Wait, what is that? The girl discovered a piece of paper and set the teapot down. She unfolded the note and read:

Hey guys,
I went to the bakery by the post office to order cake and get rolls and some of those delicious pastries.

> **It's six o'clock. I should be back within forty minutes or so.**
> **Love,**
> **Manya**

"That early bird," Anke said aloud. "Even though she went to bed after me, Manya still got up sooner. How much sleep did she get? Four, five, six hours…?" Staring at the clock, Anke raised her brows. "Wait a minute! Six o'clock? That was more than three hours ago."

"Anke?"

The girl jumped and dropped the note. She placed her hand on her chest. "Mark, you scared me!"

"I'm sorry," he said, tucking his black top into his blue jeans. "It was unintentional. Are you all right?"

"I'm okay." Pulling a red rubber band from her wrist, Anke tied her hair into a ponytail. She picked up the paper.

"What's that?" Mark asked.

"A note from Manya."

"What does it say?"

Anke read the contents aloud. Mark looked up and focused on the clock. "Wow, what's taking her so long?"

"I don't know," the girl said, sitting down. "This is so unlike her."

Mark sat next to Anke. "Let's not jump to conclusions. There's got to be some kind of explanation." He extended his hand. "May I have the paper, please?" She placed the object into his palm. Mark studied the note as if trying to find some clues.

Covering her face with her hands, Anke mumbled, "What if she had a flat tire or was in a bad wreck?"

He smoothed his hair. "Get ready and wake Heiko. I'll meet you two up front in the car. We need to look for her."

They left the kitchen. Mark stopped in the hallway and put his shoes on. Moving her hand on the railing, Anke climbed the stairs. At the top, she heard the front door shut. The girl lowered her head and followed the orange carpet to the back. She stopped at the east bedroom. As Anke reached for the handle, the door opened.

"Good morning, honey," Heiko greeted, still in pajamas. His hair was messy. He tried to kiss her on the mouth.

She turned her head sideways. "I came to wake you. We need to leave as soon as possible. Manya is missing."

"What?"

"Manya went to the bakery this morning and never returned. Mark is getting the car out, so we can look for her."

Heiko shook his head. "That's impossible! Manya is smarter and more careful than the three of us combined."

"I agree. But those traits guarantee her nothing! She still could get into a trap." Anke gave it some thought. "Remember last year, when we talked about a man with a white car snatching young girls?"

"Yeah."

"I never heard that he was caught. What if he kidnapped Manya?"

He placed his hands on her shoulders and looked into her eyes. "But Anke, that was only a rumor. Tell me, when have you last heard or seen anything about a crime on radio or television, let alone the newspapers?"

"Never."

"See, we have no crime here," Heiko said. "It's totally safe to live in East Germany and rumors are just that. Manya could be lost and might be getting help as we speak."

"A country without crime? I don't believe that for a minute! That's exactly what the government wants you to think. You're so naïve when it comes to politics," Anke said, angrily tapping herself on the forehead. His jaw dropped. He wanted to say something but decided against it. "Anyway," she calmly continued. "I still have to get ready and need to leave this for a later debate."

"I'll wait for you downstairs," Heiko said and went back inside.

Anke rushed into the room across the hallway.

Minutes later, somebody honked in front of the house. Anke and Heiko met up in the corridor. She noticed that they both wore white t-shirts and blue jeans. He truly is my soul mate, she thought and grabbed his hand. They went outside. Her eyes set on the flowers aligning the path to the gate. She remembered Manya smelling a rose upon arrival.

Heiko helped his fiancée into the backseat and joined his friend up front. He buckled up. "How do you guys know that Manya went to the bakery?" Heiko asked. "Couldn't she have gone somewhere else like the post office or so?"

"Because she left a note," Anke said.

Mark gave him the piece of paper, shifted the car into gear, and took off.

Heiko read. As he looked at his watch, his throat tightened. Four hours had passed. He put the note into his pocket and stared at the windshield. "Now I understand."

Mark parked the car in front of the bakery and took a deep breath.

Turning around, Heiko checked on his fiancée. The girl gazed at the floor, silently sobbing. He climbed into the backseat and laid his arm around her. Gently kissing Anke on the temple, he held her tight.

Mark got out. "I'll be back in a bit." He pulled on his top to remove some wrinkles, shut the door, and walked off.

9

The flat green building stretched far to the back. Various pine and deciduous trees bordered a wide driveway on the east and west side of the property. Up front, a steel rack held three bicycles. Above the display window, plastic letters assembled the word 'LIESEGANG.' Even though he had heard a lot of good things at work about the store, Mark had never gone here. Only six blocks from his house, the Schulz bakery just had always been more convenient. He walked up the steps.

A wicker basket in the window attracted his attention. Inside, white, pumpernickel, and poppy seed rolls, braids, and breads, all glazed, made an appealing display. He craved a poppy seed roll, but knew that's not what he came here for. Mark went inside.

The scent of vanilla and powdered sugar made his stomach growl. Several women and one man stood in line. Two sales associates with white aprons rushed from one end of the counter to the other, completing orders. Both women had short brown hair. Hands and nose on the glass case, a toddler stared at the doughnut section. Three women talked. He noticed the youngest chatterer had striking similarity with the boy near the doughnuts.

Mark got in line. Mmmh, he thought, I wonder if the saleswoman in her twenties or the one in her fifties will help me. He watched the older sales associate carefully scoop squares, pastries, and doughnuts onto rectangular cardboards and wrap them with white paper. Smiling, the woman handed her packages over for money. Sometimes she gave out change.

Manya crossed his mind. He brainstormed about the girl's possible whereabouts. The thought of her lying blood-covered on the side of the road gave him chills.

"Hello, what can I get for you?" the younger saleswoman asked, interrupting his train of thought.

"My name is Mark Schmidt. I urgently need to talk to

someone who worked here this morning, between six and seven."

She briefly gazed at the people behind him. "Let me get somebody." The lady disappeared into the back and returned with a gray-haired short man in a white two-piece outfit. "Come with me," she said and took Mark to a small room behind the sales area. Two tables, with four chairs each, filled the room. A picture of the Pillnitz castle in Dresden hung to his left.

The woman closed the door and pointed at one of the chairs. "Have a seat. How can I help you?"

"I'm looking for a sixteen-year-old girl. Her name is Manya Mallwitz. She has brown shoulder-length hair, is about five foot four, and weighs around a hundred ten pounds. The girl headed here this morning to buy some rolls and pastries and never returned."

"Did you say between six and seven?"

"Correct."

The woman gave it some thought. "I did help a young lady this morning, fitting that description. I'm unable to recall everything she bought, but I do remember that she got rolls and ordered some kind of cake. Could that be?"

Mark tapped himself on the forehead. "How could I forget? Manya was also ordering cake for the engagement party tonight!"

"I'll be right back." The saleswoman left. Returning, she gave him a yellow paper slip and said, "This is the order I took."

Mark checked the information. "Manya Mallwitz…yep, that's her. And as far as I know, there's only one person with that name out there." He sighed. "At least now we know that she was here. Do you recall where she was heading afterwards?"

"The young lady went east, toward the train station."

"East?" Wrinkling his forehead, he scratched the tip of his chin. "But the town is west of the bakery. That doesn't make any sense. Are you sure?"

"I'm positive. After helping your friend, I stepped outside to catch some fresh air. I watched her unchain her bike. A far train whistled, as it always does every morning at seven. The young lady looked around and noticed me at the top of the steps. She inquired about the railroad crossing. I gave her directions and she headed east."

"Did you see her after that?"

"I got busy serving customers and never saw her again."

Mark's stomach growled as he returned the order form. "Thank you," he said and rose. "I better get going. Can you by chance hold off on the cake?"

"Of course," the woman replied and guided him through a wide hallway to the back. The scent of freshly baked bread strengthened with each step. Mmmh, did he love that smell. He so wanted to devour a poppy seed roll. His stomach rumbled louder than before. The woman stopped. "Wait here," she said. As she walked through double doors, an avalanche of warm air hit his face and body. His nose tickled. He sneezed. The saleswoman returned and handed him a flat oval item, wrapped in parchment paper. "This will calm your stomach and help you think better."

I wonder what this is, Mark thought, gently squeezing the package with his thumbs. It was crispy and soft. Judging by the texture and shape, he had an idea. "Thank you," Mark said and followed the woman to the end of the hallway. The scent of fresh bread had faded. Opening a squeaky metal door, the woman showed him out. Mark shook the lady's hand. "Thank you so much for your time and the bread. Please keep an eye out for Manya and her silver Diamond bike."

"I will. If you have more questions, just ask for Barbara." She got a pencil and a blank cake order form from her right pocket. "Why don't you give me your phone number in case I see something."

"My number is two-eight-five-nine-six."

"Two…eight…five…nine…six," the lady slowly repeated while writing. "I wish you the best of luck, young man."

Using the driveway east of the building, he walked to his car.

"And?" Heiko asked as Mark got into the driver seat. Mark recollected his conversation with the saleswoman and unwrapped the package.

"What's that?" Anke asked, peeking over Mark's shoulder.

"I can't believe this!" Mark exclaimed. "She gave me poppy seed bread!" He cheerfully divided the loaf, giving one piece to Anke, one to Heiko, and keeping the last one for himself. After taking a large bite, he placed the bread in his lap and took off.

"Still warm," Anke mumbled, chewing.

"That was nice of her," Heiko noted.

Mark finished chewing. "We'll search the train station and surrounding area, then retrace Manya's route home."

Thinking, Maybe we should get out more; Anke wiped a crumb from her chin. "I didn't even know your town had a train station."

"Remember that factory job of mine?"

"Yeah."

"That's how all my assembled masterpieces get to their final destinations." He stopped at a red light and took another bite. The signal turned green. Trees, tress, everywhere trees, he thought. I can see why Manya chose to go to the train station; morning has its magic on vegetation. He remembered how Manya often surveyed his yard last year before coming in for breakfast. The dew on his roses mesmerized the girl the most.

A train whistled from a distance. As they arrived at the railroad crossing, the barriers lowered. A blue car stopped behind them. Waiting on the pedestrian walk, two women stared toward the direction of the oncoming train. A skinny German shepherd ran across the street and disappeared into the woods.

"Did you guys see that dog?" Anke asked.

"Yeah," Heiko replied. "What about it?"

"It looked lost and malnourished. We should find it and turn it in."

"Anke," her fiancé said, looking at her lips, then eyes. "I love your dedication to animals. However, you don't know this dog. What if it's aggressive and bites you? It could have rabies! Think about it. Besides, remember what we came here for."

"But what if the dog truly needs help?"

"Forget about the animal! We have other priorities right now."

Anke, disappointed, puckered her lips and gazed at the barriers. A long freight train rumbled by.

"See," Mark said, pointing at the rust-covered cars. "I bet some of my work is right in there."

"When will we tell our parents that Manya is missing?" Anke asked.

Mark turned around. "If we don't find her by the end of the afternoon, we will send telegrams, okay?"

She nodded.

Mark turned to the front. The train passed and the barriers went up. Mark quickly finished his bread, crumpled up the parchment paper, and started the car. "Ready?"

"As ever," Heiko said.

Mark parked the car near the train station. Searching the building and surrounding area and questioning countless railroad employees, they found no trace of Manya. When the group returned and got into the car, Mark looked at the couple in the backseat. He said, "I've got to tell you something."

"Did Manya and you get into an argument last night?" Anke asked.

He shook his head. "No, not at all. It's something else."

"What is it?"

"You and Heiko, I'd like you to know that I've always had feelings for Manya, somewhat like love at first sight."

"Wow, I had no idea!" Anke said, exchanging looks with her fiancé.

Heiko raised his eyebrows. "I always knew you liked her, but I would have never guessed your emotions ran that deep."

Mark sighed. "I tell you, my heart aches so much. I wish I had one more minute to share my feelings with her." He lowered his head. "Maybe she even would have never disappeared if I had told her last night."

"You need to stop thinking like that," Heiko said. "Even if you had told her, with her fascination with nature, I bet she still would have gone to all the places she went to this morning. Manya's disappearance has nothing to do with you. Don't blame yourself for things you have no control over."

"You're right, I shouldn't think this way," Mark said. He rubbed his cheek. "We better get going."

They retraced Manya's route, talked to the local fire chief, and checked with the administrator of the local hospital… without success. At the police station, everybody hesitated getting out of the car.

"Shouldn't Manya's parents do this?" Anke asked. "I mean I know her well, but what if I forget important details?"

"I just thought of the same thing," Mark said. "Let's go to the post office first and then file a report. Manya's parents need to know the situation. Who knows when the police will take action anyway? It could be hours or days."

"Hours or days," Anke said. "Why would they drag it out?"

"Because we're talking about a teenager here, not some five-year old. The police might even treat her like a runaway."

She narrowed her eyes and raised her voice. "No, they wont. I will not allow it. I'll tell them what type of person Manya really is and what I think about her disappearance."

"Pushing them will probably get you nowhere."

"I don't care! At least, they'll know what's on my mind." She loudly exhaled and leaned on Heiko. Calmer, she said, "I just hope they'll find her soon."

Mark took off.

10

No space, huh, Mark thought and passed the two-story beige building going east. He parked in the empty lot next door. They walked back. Except for the bicycle rack, post office lettering, and the white sign with the yellow horn, the building looked more like a residential home.

"What's upstairs?" Anke asked, wondering why she didn't notice all these details the day before. She remembered her exhaustion.

"I have no idea," Mark replied. "People living, I guess."

Puzzled, Anke stood in front of the building and inhaled deeply. The wind carried the scent of carnations from the flower shop west of the building. She noticed thick iron bars on the bottom windows of the post office. Those remind me of a prison in a Winnetou and Old Shatterhand movie, she thought.

"Let's go," Mark said. Passing the concrete bench they sat on the day before, the couple followed him inside. The constant talking, typewriting, stamping, doors opening and closing, shuffling, and unusual brightness from the ceiling lights created an unpleasant atmosphere. It smelled like tape, glue, ink, and paper. Four of five counters had lines, averaging a dozen customers. People came. People left.

Mark picked up three forms from the document island near the entrance and gave them to Anke. "Here, it'll be a while. Fill 'em out while we're waiting." They went in line.

"Next, please," the brunette in postal uniform at counter 2 hollered as the previous customer stepped away. The skin under her eyes looked dark and puffy. Checking the clock on the wall across from her, she yawned and forced herself to smile.

Anke placed the completed forms on the counter. "We'd like to send three urgent telegrams." She stepped back and reached for her fiancé's hand.

Nodding, the lady read the contents. Her smile faded. She

counted the words, time-stamped and priced each document, and summarized all charges. "Your total comes to eighty-four marks."

After exchanging looks with Heiko, Mark paid for the telegrams.

Anke hid her face on Heiko's chest and wept. "I'm so sorry for embarrassing us. I just can't hold it in any longer."

Putting his arms around her, her fiancé whispered, "It's okay."

The brunette rounded up the telegrams and left her cubicle. A minute passed.

"Where did she go?" Mark said, looking at the empty booth and his friends.

Another employee took the lady's spot. The man straightened his uniform and concentrated on Mark and the teenagers. "My co-worker will meet you at counter 4. She'll explain everything."

Shrugging shoulders, Mark looked at Heiko. They walked to the closed counter and waited.

The brunette approached. "Hello. I apologize for the confusion and delay. I took the telegrams to our telegraph worker and made sure that they were sent immediately. I also was supposed to get off nine minutes ago…" She glanced at the booth where she worked at earlier. "But my replacement had bicycle problems and just showed up. She extended her right hand toward Heiko and Anke. "Anyways, my name is Lydia Marro. I would like to help you."

Heiko turned to Mark. "What do you think?"

"I think we should utilize all help we can get and accept her offer."

"Okay," Heiko said and shook the lady's hand.

Lydia gently touched Anke's shoulder. "Are you all right, young lady?" The girl nodded. "Are you hungry? Would you like to have a cheese sandwich and some grapes? Somebody bought meals for all employees today, so I have an extra lunch on hand." The lady rummaged through her large purse and retrieved a white plastic lunch box. She held it toward Anke. "Here, I'd be delighted to give it to you. Food always makes me feel better."

The girl glimpsed at Heiko.

"It's totally safe, I guarantee you," Lydia said. She tapped on a red pin with a 20 on her upper chest and said, "As you can see, I'm very committed and, besides, you know where I work."

Heiko thought about the poppy seed bread. Preoccupied with the current situation, he was unaware of how many hours had gone by. His empty stomach suddenly made him nauseous. "Go ahead. A cheese sandwich is always better than nothing."

Mark introduced the teenagers and himself. As he finished talking, a door slammed in the back. A phone rang. Several items were loudly stamped at the counter to the left.

Lydia raised her voice. "Let's go outside. It's kind of noisy in here."

The group walked out. Anke sat on the all-too familiar bench in front of the building and ate Lydia's lunch.

"I'll be right back," Mark said and crossed the street. He disappeared into the Liesegang bakery.

As the girl finished her meal, Mark returned. "No news."

Anke handed the empty container to the lady. "Thank you."

"Feel any better?" Lydia asked.

"A little."

The brunette stowed the lunch box. "Now, in order for me to help you, I would like to know everything about your missing friend. Everything that comes to mind…how you met, how long you've known her, what she looks like, her character, why you're in this town, and how she went missing. It'll give me a better feel on how to go about the next step."

Mark and the teenagers took turns, talking about Manya and the yearly get-togethers. At the end, Heiko gave Manya's note to the lady and explained how Anke found it in the morning.

Lydia studied the paper and returned it. "What have you done so far?"

Mark told her about the visit with the bakery employee and the search.

Gazing from Heiko to Anke, the woman asked, "Maybe I'm missing something, but why did you travel without parents this year?"

Heiko explained, even mentioning his marriage proposal to Anke to convey his maturity.

Mark laid his hand on the woman's shoulder. "Miss Lydia, please understand that these teenagers are more responsible than a lot of adults I work with. I fully trust their judgment, especially Manya's. If something indeed happened to the girl, I'm convinced that it was an uncontrollable event or factor."

"Honestly, Manya almost backed out of the trip," Anke said and described her friend's encounters.

"Most interesting," Lydia said.

"Should we've done anything differently?" Mark asked.

"You're fine. You did exactly what you should have done."

"We planned on filing the Missing Persons report next."

"I've got a better idea," Lydia said. "Instead of waiting in line at the police station, how about having an officer come to your home?"

"Sure," Mark said.

"What's your address?"

"Main Street ten."

"Do you have a phone?"

"I do. My number is two-eight-five-nine-six."

Lydia wrote the information on a piece of paper. "Wait here. I'll be right back." She returned after a short while. "I called my brother. He'll meet us at your house in twenty minutes."

"Your brother?" Mark asked.

"Yes, he's the lead detective at the Halle police department."

Heiko and Mark, baffled, looked at each other.

Lydia got a small key from the side pocket of her purse. "Since my pedaling speed is limited, I better get going if I want to be at your house on time. I'll see you in a bit." The woman quickly walked behind the building.

11

The man in his fifties rang the bell and stared at the large 10 near the door. His dark brown suit blended well with the color of his hair and his briefcase. Perfectly centered, a light blue tie covered the buttons of the shirt underneath. Clean-shaven, the man's face was wet. As he unbuttoned his jacket, the door opened.

"Good afternoon, you must be Lydia's brother," Mark greeted. The scent of expensive cologne entered his nose. Except for the hair color, he saw no resemblance with Lydia.

"Yes, I'm Superintendent Dieter Marro." The men shook hands.

"I'm Mark Schmidt. Please come in."

The detective retrieved a handkerchief from his chest pocket and patted his face dry. "What a hot afternoon."

"Hot indeed," Mark replied, showing the visitor into the living room. He introduced his friends and pointed at the closest armchair. "Have a seat. Would you like some lemonade?"

"Sure."

Mark filled a glass and set it in front of the detective.

"Thank you," Dieter Marro said, chugging the liquid down. He removed a stapled document from his briefcase and placed it on the table. "I prefer to have parents fill this out. However, since Manya's disappearance is out of her character and time is of essence, I would like to get everything started. Once the report is filed, I can always update it."

Mark joined his friends on the couch and, with their help, completed the document. As Dieter Marro reviewed the form, the bell rang.

Mark left and returned with a man in a white coverall. "Superintendent, this is Heinrich Mallwitz, Manya's father."

"Dieter Marro," the detective said, rising. He shook Heinrich's hand, "I'm so sorry about your daughter's disappearance. I will do my best in finding her."

"…And I will help as well," Lydia said and introduced herself as the detective's sister.

Dieter Marro passed the paperwork to Manya's father. "Please see if you can add anything."

"Okay," Heinrich said, bobbing his head once. He sat next to the detective and went over the document. Forty minutes passed. Heinrich wrote something on the last page and returned the paperwork. "I've got a couple of things…first: my daughter has a heart-shaped birthmark under her left arm. And second: I don't know where this information came from, but as far as I know, Manya never took Karate. She would have told me."

"It was a well-kept secret among the four of us," Mark said. "Many times, Manya and I snuck out and practiced in the basement while everyone else was upstairs. During school months, I regularly sent material to her home. She hid the Karate stuff far under her bed and only practiced in her room when her mother and her brother were gone." He sighed. "Manya actually wanted to get certified this year and surprise everybody. Her competency test is scheduled for next week."

"She was that good?" Heinrich inquired.

Mark nodded. "I told her that a young girl like her should always know how to defend herself. Manya picked up quickly. And when the rumor popped up about a guy snatching girls, she put in even more effort."

"How did you choose Karate?"

"I initially took the sport in high school."

"Is Anke getting certified as well?"

"Except for school, I pretty much hang around Heiko most of my waking hours and figured he'd be protection enough," Anke said. "Besides, by the time I've tied up this…" She ran her fingers lengthwise through her hair. "Any attacker would have already taken control."

The phone rang. Mark answered and handed it to the detective. "For you."

"Hello," Dieter Marro said and listened. "Okay. ... I'm on my way." He gave the phone to Mark. "I've got to go. As soon as this other thing is taken care off, I'll file the report. I anticipate returning in about two hours. Your presence is critical since I need to go over a few things with you. I hope Manya's mother will have arrived by then." The detective quickly put the stapled document into his briefcase. "In the meantime, Lydia will remain here and explain her next step."

"No problem," Heinrich said. "We'll be here waiting for you."

Mark walked the detective out.

12

The evening sun peeked through the living room windows. A dog barked outside. Wearing a fuchsia pantsuit, Rosemary sat on the couch and knitted. She listened to Karat's 'Der Blaue Planet' on the radio and smiled. A few years ago, she had unsuccessfully tried to get a tape with the top chart hit for her daughter. Now, the song is still played on her favorite East German station, melting her heart with every musical note. The band couldn't have described the Earth with a better melody.

Rosemary glanced at the clock. It was past six. I better make dinner, she thought, dropping the needles and knit piece into her lap and unraveling the wool from her right index finger.

'Ding dong,' the bell echoed in the hallway.

She pushed the knitting stuff aside and rose. Did Michael forget his keys…a little early for him. Walking into the corridor, she checked the ruler-shaped key holder near the entrance. Her son's key ring was gone.

The bell rang again. Rosemary peeked through the peephole and saw a brunette in her early twenties. Two short ponytails with red ribbons hung over the stranger's ears and reminded her of her first day of school. Rosemary momentarily closed her eyes and…grinned. She took a closer look and discovered a clipboard with a large white envelope in the stranger's hands. I wonder what that is? Rosemary thought. She checked her hair in the close-by mirror and opened the door. "Good evening, may I help you?"

"Good evening, ma'am," the brunette with ponytails said. "Are you Miss Rosemary Mallwitz?"

"Yes, I am. What's this about?"

"I work for the postal delivery service and have an urgent telegram."

"An urgent telegram?" Rosemary asked, scratching her collarbone.

The brunette nodded once and handed her the envelope. "Have a good evening now."

"You too," Rosemary said and closed the door. She went into the kitchen, grabbed a small knife from the counter, and sliced the envelope open. A bad feeling crept up on her like a venomous snake. She read:

+ Manya did not return from bakery this morning + search unsuccessful + will file report + come quickly + Anke +

Her stomach turned into a knot. She sank into the nearest chair. Manya is missing? Rosemary thought, shaking her head. No, that can't be true. Her fingers trembled as she read the telegram a second time. Her throat tightened. She envisioned her daughter tied up in some strange musty basement. Somebody came into the house.

"Hi Mom, I'm home," her son loudly said. He hummed a tune while opening and closing several doors in the hallway.

Michael entered the kitchen. "Mom? You look distraught. What's going on?" He noticed the paper in her hands. The layout looked familiar. Observing the envelope on the table, he said, "Is that another telegram?"

"Yes."

"What does it say?" Michael asked, sitting across from her. She pushed the paper toward him.

Lowering his head, he studied the telegram. "Is this a joke?"

His mother shook her head.

"That's impossible!" he shouted. "Manya can't be missing! She's too good of a person. Besides, she promised to be careful and she always keeps her word. Always!"

"I don't know what to tell you."

Remembering his nightmare, he jumped up and ran out of the kitchen. A door slammed in the corridor.

Several minutes passed. *What am I going to do now?*

Rosemary thought. While one child is missing, the other one is disturbed. After brooding for several moments, she decided to check on Michael. She knocked on her son's bedroom door. "Michael? Are you okay?"

"No!" he shouted and sniveled.

She entered.

Huddled in his blanket, Michael lay on the bed and stared at the round light fixture on the ceiling. A narrow trail of tears marked the side of his head and moistened the hair around his temple.

Rosemary sat on the bed and stroked her son's cheek. "I'm sure we'll find her."

"How?" he asked. "Where would we start? We don't even have a car!"

"Mark and your father do, and I'm sure we all will work together. Think positive!"

He sobbed. "Except for crying, I have difficulties doing anything at the moment. I just don't understand. Why Manya? Why us?" He paused and looked at his mother. "This is all my fault! I should have never let her go."

"Michael, this is not your fault, and don't you even think that for one second!"

"Oh, Mom," he murmured, sitting up. Tears rolled down his cheeks.

Rosemary put her arms around him and gently rocked her upper body. "Shhh."

The bell rang.

"I better answer that," his mother whispered and left. She opened the front door. A blonde in a jeans outfit stood outside. Thick hair covered her shoulders. Thin lines bordered her eyes and her lips.

"Regina!" Rosemary exclaimed. "Come in."

"Have you by chance received a telegram from Anke?" her friend inquired.

"Yes, about twenty-five minutes ago."

"I am so sorry," she said and embraced Rosemary for several moments. "My heart goes out to you."

Rosemary sighed. "Gotta keep my hope up."

"Good idea to stay positive. Can I make you some sandwiches, tea, or help with anything else? Something?"

"I think we're all right for now," Rosemary said.

Regina Radtke glanced at the floor near the entrance. "I assume you haven't packed yet?"

"Haven't even thought about it. We've been trying to cope with the news."

"Is Michael in his room?"

"Yes," Rosemary said and focused on the door at the end of the hallway. She loudly exhaled.

"He's not taking it lightly, is he?"

"Nope. Poor guy was blaming himself. I put a quick stop to that."

Regina sighed. "I wish Hubert was still alive. Even though husbands will never replace mothers, they still have the biggest shoulder to cry on."

"Yeah, he was a good man and most likely would have let us all cry on his shoulders," Rosemary said and faintly smiled.

"When do you think you'll head out?"

"Hard to say, depends on how long our errands will take. The packing will be easy."

"What kind of errands?"

"First: I've got to call my boss, requesting emergency vacation. And second: Michael has to stop at George's to tell him that he won't be over for a while. Michael, George, and George's parents were actually planning on going to the Berlin wave pool tomorrow."

"Oh, I see. Do you have enough change for the phone booth?"

"I'm sure I do. If not, I can always borrow some coins from Michael. Are you all packed?"

"No, not yet. I wanted to check on you first. But I need to

get going...."

Rosemary followed Regina outside. "You know, no matter how long it'll take or how hard it will be, nothing can hold me back from finding my daughter."

"With that attitude, you definitely will succeed."

"Let's meet on the bus in two hours to be on the safe side."

"All right, I'll save you some seats," Regina said.

"Too bad that Heiko's parents went on that cruise yesterday. They would have scooped us up, and we would've been at Mark's in no time."

"I know."

Rosemary walked her friend to the bicycle and hugged her. "Thanks for caring and being there for me. It means more than you'll ever know."

"That's what friends are for."

"You better get going, or none of us will leave town tonight."

After watching Regina take off, she went inside.

13

The lowering sun gave surrounding clouds a touch of orange. It was comfortably warm. Regina, Rosemary, and Michael approached Mark's house, each carrying a large piece of luggage.

"The roses sure have grown since I was here last," Regina said, leading the other two up the steps.

Loudly exhaling, Rosemary set her suitcase down and rubbed her right hand. "Well, I think my suitcase grew tonight as well; it seemed heavier with each step." She expected some kind of reaction from her son, but Michael only stared at the ground. He looked tired. "Did you know that Mark has some Basque ancestry?" Rosemary asked her friend. "He mentioned that in one of his letters to Manya."

"That doesn't really surprise me," Regina replied. "What does surprise me is that he's going toward his thirties and has never been married."

"His job might prevent him getting acquainted with anyone."

Or he's got a crush on Manya and nobody knows about it, Regina thought and rang the bell. A car door shut. Turning around, the women and the boy saw a man in a brown suit approaching.

Rosemary whispered, "Who's that?"

"Have no idea," Regina replied as the door opened.

"Hello," Mark greeted with a monotone voice and embraced the visitors. "I'm so sorry about Manya's disappearance," he said to Rosemary. "I wish there was something I could do." Picking up her suitcase, Mark noticed Dieter Marro walking up the steps. He signaled to follow inside. After getting Regina's luggage, Mark gave a brief introduction. The detective expressed his compassion to Rosemary. Making clear he understood that Manya was not a runaway, Dieter Marro assured that he'd do his best to find her. Mark, Rosemary, Michael, Regina, and the detective went into the living room.

"Dad!" Michael shouted, discovering his father. He hugged him. Sitting on the ledge of Heinrich's armchair, he talked about his nightmare.

Anke rushed to Regina. "Oh, Mom," she said and sobbed. "I missed you so much. I'm having such a tough time."

Holding her daughter, she softly stroked her back. "I am so sorry that you have to go through something like this. I wish I could bear your pain."

"I don't know what to do."

"Take one day at a time and never give up," Regina said.

"I'll try."

Greeting Rosemary, Regina, and Michael, Lydia introduced herself. She departed.

The detective gave a stapled document to Rosemary. "Ms. Mallwitz, this is a copy of the Missing Persons report that I filed on your daughter. Please look it over for missing information and inconsistencies." The woman nodded. Turning to Heiko, Dieter Marro said, "I also need to submit Manya's note into evidence. Do you still have that?"

"Yes, I do," he replied, retrieving the paper from his back pocket.

"May I see?" Rosemary asked.

"Sure," the detective said and gave her the note.

Studying the paper, she noticed that it truly was her daughter's handwriting…truly, Manya's last contact to people close to her. Rosemary yearned to keep the note. Heavyhearted, she bit her lip and returned it.

Dieter Marro read the paper and stored it in his briefcase.

Rosemary went over the stapled document. The only discrepancy she could find was the Karate. Mark's explanation kindled a stronger hope that her daughter will be found alive.

"According to the Missing Persons report, Manya has pierced ears," said the detective, "did she by chance wear any earrings this morning?"

"Manya didn't wear or bring any jewelry this time," Anke replied. "Until certification, she and Mark were going to practice Karate every afternoon, starting tomorrow. Jewelry on, jewelry off; earrings in, earrings out; it was just too much for her, she told me."

A minute of silence passed.

"Detective Marro, how long do you think it will take to find my daughter?" Rosemary asked.

"Hard to tell. It depends on overall circumstances. Each case is different. It could take days, weeks, months, or even years."

"Years? Could Manya still be alive then?"

"Possibly, but like I said: each case is different." Dieter Marro retrieved a pen and a notebook from his briefcase. "I have a few more questions for you and Mr. Mallwitz before wrapping this up. By all means, please do not be offended. This is standard procedure and will only help with the investigation."

"Okay," Rosemary said. Heinrich nodded.

Thinking about Michael's joy when discovering his father, the detective asked, "Am I correct in assuming you live in separate households?"

"Yes," Rosemary replied.

"Is either side of the family wealthy or about to inherit a large amount of western currencies like British pounds, west marks, or dollars?"

She looked at her ex-husband who shook his head. "No."

"Any relatives living or temporarily working in a capitalist country like West Germany or the United States of America?"

"Not on my side," Rosemary said.

"Mine neither," Heinrich replied.

"Any connections to a capitalist country in or outside the family?"

Manya's father and mother simultaneously shook their heads.

"What are your current occupations?"

"I'm a schoolteacher," Rosemary said.

"And I'm a supervisor in construction," Heinrich replied.

"Always held the same job?"

"I have," Manya's mother answered.

"I did too until my recent promotion," Manya's father said.

"Are you both single?"

"I am," Rosemary replied.

Attracting looks, Heinrich thought of his wife before answering, "I remarried a few years ago."

"What does your spouse do? Does her family have a lot of money?"

"My wife is a registered nurse, and her family only owns a small dairy farm. That's about it. What are you getting at? Do you think Manya might have been kidnapped?"

The detective went over several scenarios in his head and said, "With given information and no current ransom demand, I believe I now can safely rule a monetary or politically motivated kidnapping out."

"Since Manya rode a new bike and Heiko, Mark, and I already checked the only local hospital and fire station without success, could we also rule an accident out?" Anke asked.

"I would refrain from that; accidents are always a possibility."

Heinrich cleared his throat. "May I ask you a few questions?"

"Sure," Dieter Marro replied.

"When did you become superintendent?"

"My supervisor promoted me about fifteen years ago after I worked on his crime scene unit for a decade."

"What did you do before that?"

"I was on the cold case squad for several years."

"And prior to that?"

"I patrolled streets."

"I bet you gained a lot of knowledge over the years," Regina said.

"Definitely. It was all out there. All I had to do is reach for it. Criminal investigations, science, and forensics have always drawn me in."

"Do you ever get nightmares from your cases?" Michael asked.

"I used to get 'em a lot when I worked on the cold case squad. But I haven't had any for a long time. I bet it's been a dozen years."

"What were you working on?"

"I apologize, but I'm unable to disclose that information, young man. I hope you understand."

Michael nodded. "Do you have a badge?"

"I certainly do."

"May I see?"

"Sure," the detective said, opening his briefcase. He pulled a black bound booklet from a small compartment near the handle, flipped it open, and held it toward Michael.

"That's it?"

"That's my badge," Dieter Marro assured.

"I always thought badges were made of metal and star-shaped."

"The identification booklets are all we've got here." Dieter Marro smiled. "You must be thinking of a sheriff badge in some Wild West movie."

"May I take a closer look and hold it?"

The detective bobbed his head and passed the booklet to the boy.

Michael glided his fingers over the black material. "Is this leather?"

"I don't think so. It's some kind of other, more durable material."

"Even though your badge is not what I thought it would be, I still think it's kind of cool. I wish I owned one. I would carry it around and show it off to all my family and friends and whoever wants to see it."

"You'll need to earn it."

"When can I start?"

"No," Dieter Marro chuckled. "It's not like that. You've got to earn it by completing an apprenticeship, getting accepted into a department like the traffic or state trooper division, completing the appropriate police academy course, and, most importantly, you have to be eighteen when you apply."

"Seems complicated," Michael said and returned the booklet.

"It's not as hard as it sounds. Just like Lydia, I started at the post office. Look where I'm at now. I made it and so can you, if that's your heart's desire." The detective stowed his badge.

"How are you planning on finding my girl?" Heinrich asked.

"Even though I'm unable to give out specific details, I guarantee you that I'll utilize all my expertise and any other resources I can get my hands on. I will also work overtime, including weekends. If you have any doubts about my dedication, just ask my boss or my sister."

"You've got to find Manya," Rosemary said. "I want her home."

"Ms. Mallwitz, I promise that I will find your daughter, and when I do, you'll be the first to know."

"How many missing children have you located?" Heinrich inquired.

"I'm unable to disclose that information."

"Do you know how it feels to have a missing child?"

The detective gazed at Michael and said, "In matter of fact, I do."

"How so? Through your cases?"

"No, in real life."

Heinrich, baffled, stared at the man across from him. His tone became friendlier, "You mean you went through something like this yourself? Is that the reason you became a detective?"

"I was already on the crime scene unit when all that came

down…." Dieter Marro exhaled aloud and focused on his right palm as his left thumb and index finger slowly rotated a wedding band. "Seventeen years ago."

"What happened?" Rosemary asked.

"My wife and daughter went missing."

"Were they kidnapped?"

"That was my first thought since my wife's family was well off, and we accumulated quite a bit of money and large gifts over the years. But then, after hours of search, my father-in-law located the burned wreckage and bodies in the forest. Investigators concluded that the pilot had suffered a severe heart attack."

Chewing on her thumbnail, Anke asked, "Wouldn't somebody have seen the explosion or fire?"

"Under normal circumstances, yes," the detective replied. "However, at the estimated time of the crash, a severe thunderstorm swept the area, making a detection nearly impossible."

"The fact that your family wasn't kidnapped and that you know what happened to them gives you some kind of closure, doesn't it?" Regina asked.

Dieter Marro watched Mark leave. Giving it some thought, he said, "That day, part of me died in that forest. Nothing could ever bring my family back. If my parents and the in-laws hadn't removed my wife's and my daughter's belongings from my house, I'd still look at them today. I can't fathom that I'll ever get over them being gone. Would you call that closure?"

"I am so sorry about your loss, detective. You have my deepest sympathy and respect."

"How did Lydia take the news?" Anke asked.

"She was an emotional wreck for several weeks and vowed never to get married. To this day, Lydia hasn't walked down an aisle yet."

"How old was your daughter?" Rosemary inquired.

"Five."

"So little. Why did they go in the first place, if I may ask?"

"Just the night before, my wife found out that she was expecting again. She was so excited. Nothing could have stopped her from sharing the life-changing news with her family in person."

Mark entered with a large tray, containing a big teapot, spoons, tea glasses, plates, a small bowl with sugar cubes, and a large platter with cheese and salami sandwiches. Regina distributed the dishes, spoons, and tea.

"Why didn't you go?" Regina asked.

"My wife didn't want to wait until I got off work." He paused and watched hot steam escape the tilted lid of the teapot. "I so wish I had gone, or at least prevented her from going on that day."

"Did you say your daughter passed away seventeen years ago?" Anke asked.

"Yes," the detective replied, drinking some tea and taking a cheese sandwich from the platter.

"That's the same year Manya and I were born: nineteen sixty-eight!"

"Kind of odd," Regina noted, raising her brows.

Nineteen sixty-eight, Rosemary thought. Memories of her pregnancy and Manya's first few weeks of life popped up. She smiled, blew on her tea, and took a sip.

Dieter Marro stashed pen and notebook into his briefcase and closed it. With a serious look, he said, "I would like to talk about confidentiality now. This pertains to everybody in this room." He waited until all eyes were set on him. "Manya's disappearance and related information may not be made public. Nothing will leave this room; today, tomorrow, or the days after."

Regina's mouth opened. Perplexed, she exchanged looks with Rosemary.

"What about family and friends?" Heiko asked.

The detective shook his head.

Scratching his cheek, Heinrich asked, "Are you telling me

that I'm unable to freely express myself? This is unacceptable! I feel like I'm signing off on my daughter as if she never existed. How do you expect to make any progress or to find the girl under such conditions? Will you be combing the woods by yourself? Is a search even on your agenda? Is this even legal? What about Lydia? Is she actually going to meet and help us tomorrow? The whole thing is a sham!"

"I understand how frustrating this may be, but let me explain a few things," Dieter Marro said calmly. "First of all: you're not signing off on Manya. You just can't make the situation known to others. Second: please understand that confidentiality is not my personal request but a government order. I follow strict protocol. Third: what Lydia says she does; so expect her to be there tomorrow. Fourth: whether you realize it or not, you are fortunate that I already made an exception in allowing Lydia to help you. And fifth and last: I have an excellent track record and was recognized as one of the best detectives in the nation. Therefore, I believe that I have the skills to find your daughter."

"I respect your dedication and case history," Heinrich said. "But what if Manya was the victim of a crime? With your confidentiality doctrine, could you even protect others? People have the right to know what's going on in their community and country. Does the government care?" He rose and pointed at Anke. "What about her? Couldn't she be the next victim?"

Regina moved her chair closer to her daughter and grabbed her hand.

"My daughter is a human being and so are her friends and everybody else in this country," Manya's father said. "A cover up is a cover up, no matter how you put it. It's plain and simple corruption and should be deemed a crime. Just like perpetrators, members of the government should be prosecuted for each homicide victim they could have prevented."

Dieter Marro wondered if Manya's father could become physical. Sweat collected on his forehead and ran down his face. The salty liquid stung his eyes. Drying his face and forehead, he debated what to do next. He urged to grab his briefcase and run, but decided against it.

"Heinrich, please," Rosemary begged, defensively raising her hands toward her ex-husband. "The man is only doing his job and has been through enough. Give him a break!"

"I agree," Regina said. "Heinrich, you need to stop." Manya's father took a deep breath and sat down. He rubbed his face.

"Are you okay?" Rosemary asked the detective. "You look awfully pale."

"I'm all right."

"Detective Marro, I apologize," Heinrich said calmly. "I never meant to stir my anger toward you and know that you're only doing what you were told. Please don't take it personal."

"It's okay; you're not the first and won't be the last to react this way. We all have our differences, especially during difficult situations like this. You're only human." Rising, the detective extended his hand toward Manya's father. "No hard feelings."

The men shook hands.

"I give you my word as a gentleman," Dieter Marro said, sitting down. "No matter what, I will solve Manya's case."

"We trust that you will," Regina said.

"May I ask a question?" Anke inquired.

The detective nodded.

"Somebody in school told me that the government makes people disappear, is that true?"

"I'm not in the position to answer that."

"What happens if you don't comply with the regulations? Couldn't a disappearance be one of those consequences?"

"First: I most likely will kiss my job good-bye, and then… who knows what."

"So, you're pretty much in the same position we are," Regina said.

"Possibly."

"Have you ever killed someone?" Mark asked.

Stretching his left shoulder, Dieter Marro felt the fabric strap holding the pistol under his shirt. "I drew my gun a few times but never had to use it."

"Ever been shot at?"

"Thankfully not."

Anke sighed. "I'm still in disbelief that Manya just disappeared. I feel like I'm in a dream in hope of waking up."

"Maybe we should inquire with the owner of that forest near the train station," Heiko said.

The detective shook his head. "I would strongly discourage that."

Rosemary glanced at her son. He looked so much like his father. In a few years, he might even be wearing the same size of clothing. Puberty can do wonders on a child's body. As a long-time teacher, she had seen plenty over the years, including the changes on her own daughter. However, Michael's upcoming hormonal turbulence concerned her. What if Michael had to grow up without his sister? Would he be stabile enough to pull through without problems? Her heart ached.

The detective wrote Heinrich's and Rosemary's contact information down. "If anything comes up, I'll let you know." He grabbed his suitcase and rose. "This concludes my visit. Thank you for the tea and the sandwich."

Along with Michael, Rosemary and Regina walked the detective out and watched him take off.

Lydia met Manya's family and friends the next day. Together, they combed street after street, alley after alley. Lydia assured that she had a lot of connections and would conduct more searches in the coming days. Repeatedly, she emphasized to keep up hope. However, the detective's and Lydia's efforts turned out to be fruitless. Manya seemed to have vanished into thin air. Several months went by.

14

Heavy snow covered the dense forest aligning the road. The sparkling crystals and majestic trees put him in the Christmas spirit. He imagined his wife of three years decorating a young spruce with colorful bulbs and candles in their living room. In his early twenties, he couldn't wait to become a family and proposed to her quickly. Within six months, they were married. Now, his black coverall could hardly hide the big belly from the delicious, homemade food his wife had been making ever since. He was happy.

Slowing his truck down, he observed the trees on the left. Two red squirrels attracted his attention. Shaking branches and dropping globs of snow, the animals chased each other from tree to tree. They disappeared. He carefully drove through the open gate that was a little wider than a street lane. A high fence enclosed the deposit site and stretched over several acres. It took him a while to get to his destination and dump his load. He loved the money and the ash mountains that reminded him of giant multi-colored sand castles, but dreaded the deadlines.

Turning right, he remained close to the fence. An empty dump truck approached. The driver nodded as he passed toward the gate. In a distance, he saw two skid loaders push the other truckload into a bigger pile. His vehicle stalled.

"Darn it!" he yelled and glanced at the skid loaders. "I'm so close!" The temperature in his cabin dropped drastically. His breath turned into steam. They should have listened to Maik when he told 'em it was time for replacements, he thought. Rubbing his hands together, he checked all the windows. "Oh, those cheapskates. They could have at least fixed those cracked rubber seals around the windowpanes."

He obtained a pair of work gloves from the dashboard compartment and pulled them over his own. Pushing and pulling several buttons and handles, the man tried to get his vehicle going. Not one sound came from the motor. He released the hood and leaped into the cold. A strong wind skimmed his load, carrying ashes passed the cabin. He coughed.

A skid loader pulled up. "Need any help?" a gray-haired man in his sixties shouted.

"My engine just stalled…can't do anything."

The older driver turned his vehicle off and got out. "Barely out of high school and already causing problems, huh? Those young whippersnappers!" The man smirked and pulled the collar of his work jacket up. "Let's see if I can find the problem."

"What about the deadline?" the younger driver asked.

"Forget the deadline! We'll lose time, regardless if I fix it or not. Besides, it could be something simple like a sparkplug." As the older man approached, he tripped over something. "What in the world?" Turning around, he carefully touched the object with his foot. "What is this? Feels like a frozen bag of cement. Come and help me move the snow."

The younger man shook his head. "I don't like this idea a bit. What if the boss catches us?"

"Come on, what difference would a little hand-shoveling make? Two minutes? Besides, aren't you a bit curious?"

"Yes, but…."

"All right then," the older driver said. "It's settled."

The younger man rolled his eyes and crouched across. "I only hope we're not holding everything up for a bag of bricks or a dead deer."

"Our dog-sized red deer and this?" The older man pointed at the three-meter fence. "I highly doubt that."

The younger man scooped some snow aside and paused. "They could jump that. Don't you think?"

A truck stopped. "Hey, what's going on here?" a skinny bald man yelled, leaning out. "Have you two forgotten our deadline?"

"I told you," the younger driver mumbled under his breath.

"I'm sorry, boss," the older driver said. "Pete's engine stalled and when I walked toward his truck to help him, I tripped over this...." He pointed at the bulge in the snow.

"What is it?" the bald man asked.

"Our guess is as good as yours," the older driver replied. "We just started moving the snow. What do you want us to do?"

After giving it some thought, the bald man jumped out. He pulled a black knit hat from the chest pocket of his coverall and put it on. "Well, since you've already started and I've always been of curious nature, I'd say let's at least finish the job and see what it is."

The men freed a light pink object with partial red discoloration.

"What is that?" the bald man asked.

The younger driver suddenly stumbled backwards. Placing his hand on his chest, he turned his head and disposed of his stomach contents. Hunched over, he stood and waited as if he expected another round at any moment.

Widening his eyes, the older driver stared at the discovery. "Uhm, boss...it's...it's a torso...a human torso."

"What?" his boss asked, stepping closer. He looked at the object and backed off. "No, no way...can't be! Who'd do such a thing?"

"Savages."

The bald man took a deep breath and gathered himself for a few moments. He glanced at the younger employee. "Are you all right?"

"Yes," the man replied, cleaning his face with a handkerchief.

"Listen up," the bald man said. "Here's the plan...." He pointed at the younger driver. "Pete, you stay here. Make sure that nobody touches anything or comes near. Do your best to keep the rest of your stomach contents to yourself."

"Okay."

The bald man focused on the older driver. "Egon, you notify the others to cease work. Put Tim in charge. He needs to keep the men in line while you close and guard the gate. Give only access to law officers or officials of GEL Manufacturing. In the meantime, I'll contact authorities and my supervisor. Whoever did this knew that we were going to fill up this part of the site today. The perpetrator could be anybody; you, me, them…" he pointed at the skid loaders. "And he might even be watching us right now. At the worst, he might try to destroy evidence. We can not allow that."

"If the workers question me, what do I tell 'em?" the older driver asked.

"Advise them that you're unable to disclose any information and that I'll be by in a bit with further instructions."

"How long do I stay at the gate?"

"Until a member of the authorities or I give you consent to leave."

"All right," the older driver said. He and the bald man took off.

It began to snow. Flake after flake settled on the torso. He looked ahead. The two skid loaders now stood motionless near the fence. No men were in sight. He inspected the nearby forest for anything unusual. Nothing. He felt lonely. Staring at the human remains, he wondered what happened. Loving the news, he hadn't heard of a missing person. In fact, nothing was ever broadcasted like that. He held his breath. What if this was my wife, he thought and felt his heart cramp up. This got to be somebody's loved one. Only seeing the back of the torso, it was hard to tell the gender. Cold air nipped on his toes. Shivering, he hopped into his truck and wished he at least had a blanket.

Sirens drew near. As a police car stopped behind his truck, he climbed out. Two men in uniform approached. They were quite the contrast: the younger officer was short, skinny, and blond, whereas the other one was tall, heavy, and brown-haired.

"I'm Deputy Peter Larsen," the short officer said. He pointed at his partner. "This is Sheriff Arnold Behrens. We'll be securing the site until the crime scene unit arrives. What's your name, Sir?"

"Pete Muller."

"You work for GEL Manufacturing?"

"Yes."

"May I see some identification?"

"Sure," the man in the coverall replied. The deputy's piercing eyes made him uneasy, despite his clear conscience. He wanted to look away but didn't dare to. Going back into the cabin, he retrieved his employee ID and his driver's license. He returned.

Peter Larsen checked the information and gave the documents back. Taking notes, he asked a series of questions.

Pete Muller wondered why he was being interrogated like a suspect. He was cold. His coverall felt wet. He wanted to go home. A twisted thought arose: what if the police or his boss forgot to release him? He could die of hypothermia right here, next to the torso. Now he really wanted to get home.

Peter Larsen closed his notebook. "This concludes…" Tires squealed and spun near the gate. The men turned around. A large dark blue car was stuck. After repeated tries, the vehicle moved forward and entered the ash deposit site. What if this car runs us over? Pete Muller thought. I got to quit thinking negative. This cold is just driving me crazy.

Approaching, the vehicle slowed down. After veering to the left, veering to the right, straightening, the car stopped behind his truck. He recognized the model from the news: the president rides in one of those.

A whiff of burned rubber passed.

"Another GEL employee?" the deputy inquired.

"Not sure," Pete Muller replied. "Never seen this Volvo before. Wait," he said, observing the two men getting out. "The bald man is my boss. The other one…I have no clue."

The men approached. Peter Larsen introduced himself and the sheriff.

"Michael Klein, GEL supervisor for the ash deposit site," the bald man said.

The other man shook the deputy's hand. "Ulrich Frankfurter, director of operations. I couldn't believe my ears when Klein called and said that workers found a human torso. I came as fast as I could. In all these years I worked for the company, I've never run across anything like this." He stepped to his right and searched the ground behind the officers and Pete Muller. He saw nothing but snow. "Where is it?"

"Please stay where you are," Peter Larsen said.

Gazing at the sheriff, Ulrich Frankfurter said, "Arnold, help me here."

"No can do," the sheriff said, shaking his head.

Several marked and unmarked police vehicles arrived. While patrol officers guarded the property and surrounding area, investigators, the K-9 unit, and the coroner crowded the discovery. The deputy gave Pete Muller's statements to a detective.

After an intense questioning, all GEL employees were released.

Sheriff Behrens and Deputy Larsen watched the activities. An hour went by. As they headed to the car, heavy breathing approached from behind. The officers crossed looks.

"What's that?" Sheriff Behrens asked.

Peter Larsen shrugged his shoulders. "...No idea."

The men turned around. Arnold Behrens almost tripped over a German shepherd. Sniffing the sheriff's shoes, the animal raised its hair on the back.

"Watch it!" Arnold Behrens yelled at the tall uniformed man holding the leash. Like the dog's hair on the back, the K-9 officer's black hair stood up. The man's stern look and three-centimeter haircut reminded the deputy of a soldier. "Instead of bothering us, shouldn't your dog be sniffing something more important?" Arnold Behrens asked.

The K-9 officer relaxed his facial expression. "I...I don't know what to tell you. I'm as much flabbergasted as you are."

"Is your dog male?"

"Yes."

"That explains it!" the sheriff exclaimed. "I've got two females in heat at home. Their scent must have attracted him."

"I don't know. I've never had such an encounter before."

"Animals can change, believe me. One of mine did. I ended up putting him down."

"Timo is fully trained and has been certified for several years. Why would he suddenly modify his behavior?"

"Who knows.…"

The K-9 officer thought for a moment and pulled the dog away. Patting the animal on the back, he said, "It's okay. Good boy." He straightened his posture and looked at the sheriff. "I apologize. Just ignore him."

"All right," Arnold Behrens replied and turned to the deputy. "Let's go!"

Peter Larsen and the sheriff took off.

15

Head lowered, Dieter Marro unbuttoned his brown wool coat and walked into his office. Hanging the garment on a hook near the door, he felt sweaty. He wiped his face and discovered his boss in the brown armchair across from his desk. Pins, medals, and a gold rope decorated the other man's uniform. Black-rimmed glasses, gray hair, and the sagging skin under his chin certainly confirmed the lieutenant's age of sixty-one. But his looks were deceiving in regards to his abilities. Keeping his eyes in check, working out, and shooting at a private range, he had beaten many officers in the department at competitions and mandatory drills.

That old fox, Dieter Marro thought. He wrinkled his forehead and greeted, "Good morning, lieutenant. You usually have me come to your office. What's the urgency?"

He handed him a paper. "They found your girl."

"Alive?"

His boss shook his head. "Captain Clark is on his way with her remains."

Turning as white as his office walls, the detective sat behind his desk. His chair squeaked. He stared at the facsimile in his hands. "All these months…every single day I woke up and thought 'Today is the day we find Manya.' …Now this?" Shaking his head, he thought about the loss of his own daughter. "My heart is filled with anger and helplessness. I would have given anything to find that young woman. What did I do wrong?"

"I believe you did everything you could," the lieutenant said. "You're a successful detective. Even the best have good and bad cases. Don't beat yourself up. You can't save the world. Besides, you know the statistics: the longer a person is missing, the lesser the chance of survival."

"Maybe I should have worked harder," Dieter Marro said, gazing at a framed 'Thank you' note on the wall to his right. He had successfully located the other family's son; why did he fail this case? He sighed. "Do you realize that Manya was born the same year my wife and daughter were killed?"

"Maybe you've gotten a little too attached to the case?"

"How couldn't I? How couldn't anybody? This teenager was everything any parent could have ever wanted in a child. She was helpful, honest, intelligent, and understanding; a beautiful person inside and out. Why did she have to die? I don't understand this world anymore."

"Marro," the lieutenant said and snapped his finger. "Snap out of it! She probably was already gone before we even started looking for her. What happened has happened. You can't change the past."

Putting the facsimile down, the detective buried his head into his palms. "Oh, man…."

"Even though you're unable to redirect the past, you do have the power to change the future."

Dieter Marro looked up. "Change the future? My family and Manya are dead! They aren't coming back and nothing can change that. My friendship with Rosemary is most likely dead as well since I failed to find her daughter alive or protect her. So please, don't talk about the future."

"You're looking at life from a very narrow perspective. You have the power to change the future because you catch and lock up criminals and, therefore, prevent further harm to society. Stop for a moment and think. The girl's perpetrator might even be a serial killer. What if you were the only person who could stop this case from repeating?"

The detective frowned. He rotated his gold wedding band over and over again. The lieutenant removed his hat, combed his hair with his hand, and put the hat back on. "Remember what you said when you started working for me: your job was your calling-your life? You sure have proven that to me. You've cracked all those cases, no matter how complicated, and were even recognized as one of the best in the nation." His boss pointed at the framed certificate next to the 'Thank you' note. "People envy you!"

Dieter Marro impartially shrugged his shoulders. "So?"

"You know that I'm retiring next year?"

"Yes."

"I had a meeting with the board last week," his boss said and loudly inhaled. "I suggested you as my replacement."

"What?"

"You heard me. Continue your successful route, broaden your perspective, and I'll do my best to help you land the promotion of a lifetime."

Dieter Marro widened his eyes. "I…I don't know what to say."

"Cheer up and keep moving forward."

The lieutenant approached and patted him on the back. "On that note, let's refocus. Captain Clark should be here soon. What are you doing in the next few days or evenings? We need to notify the girl's family."

"I actually was planning on meeting Rosemary tomorrow at six. Ever since her daughter went missing, I kept in touch with her on a monthly basis. She unexpectedly called yesterday and invited me over for dinner for the very first time."

"Dinner? You're way too attached!" His boss smirked. "But I guess I'll keep you on the case."

"That's comforting."

"Funny stuff aside. I hope the coroner processes the remains soon. For now, let's keep your meeting with Ms. Mallwitz for tomorrow. Try to set up an appointment with the girl's father on the same day to keep things simple. I'll get two officers lined up for tomorrow at five. Leave a message with my secretary when you'll meet with Mr. Mallwitz, so I can round up escorts for that visit as well."

"Mario, wait!" somebody shouted in the hallway. The phone rang.

Dieter Marro answered and handed the phone to his boss.

"Lieutenant Smirnov. … Yes … okay … thanks." He hung

up. "Gotta go. Captain Clark has arrived and is ready to meet me for breakfast. I expect to hear from you."

"Yes, sir," the detective said and watched his boss leave. Opening his notebook, he picked up the phone and dialed a number.

16

The rumbling freight elevator stopped and opened. Waist-high dents and scratches on the door and frame reminded of gurneys that went off course or had been trapped. I'm sure glad this isn't a hospital, Dieter Marro thought and stepped into the basement. The funky odor from the elevator strengthened and gave him goose bumps. His friend calls it the 'Smell of Death.' From that perspective, he preferred a hospital. He turned left. Waist-high punctures and scuffmarks in the brittle mortar on both sides could have anyone guess the route to the coroner's office.

The detective stopped in front of an oversized steel door. A panel with a red, green, and black button and a white plastic circle with holes hung on the wall to his right. Dieter Marro pushed the black button and leaned toward the plastic circle. "I'm here!" The door clicked and opened. He entered. A light draft tugged on his hair and clothing until the door automatically closed. He observed the room. The wardrobe closet near the door to the other room was open. Several coats and a scarf hung inside. The radio, fridge, teakettle, electrical stove, small sink, and narrow overhead cupboards hadn't changed. He discovered a burgundy couch to his left. Two matching pillows, a blue comforter, and an empty bag of chips topped the right cushion. This hasn't been here before, he thought.

A stocky man came from the adjacent room, wearing boots, scrubs, facemask, goggles, and blood-covered gloves. A hood covered his hair. He tossed the gloves into the nearby garbage can. Pushing his facemask and goggles to his neck, the man said, "Good to see you."

They shook hands.

"I'm glad to see you too, Ralf," the detective said.

"Did you fly down here? It seems we got off the phone just seconds ago."

Dieter Marro smiled.

His friend put his hood down, revealing thick red hair. "How long has it been?"

"About a year when I received my detective award."

"Yeah, I remember now. Can I make you a coffee or tea?"

"Tea sounds good."

After a short search, Ralf located two teabags in the back of his cupboards. He read the tags. "You're in luck: one mint left." His friend put the teabags in cups, filled his teakettle with water and placed it on the miniature stove.

Dieter Marro sat on the couch. Bouncing once and pushing on the neighboring cushion and pillows, he said, "Every time I visit, you seemed to have settled more down here. First, you added the closet, then the fridge and radio, then the sink, teakettle, and electrical stove, then the cupboards, and now you even have a couch with two pillows and a comforter. What's going to pop up next? Your bed?"

"With all the overtime, my bunker almost feels like a second home. Since I eat most of my meals here and occasionally take naps at lunch or dinnertime, I naturally want it cozy."

Drops of water loudly evaporated on the heated hotplate, "Hsss."

"I guess I should have wiped it down," Ralf said. The teakettle whistled. His friend turned the stove off, poured water over the teabags, and gave one of the cups to him.

Dieter Marro deeply inhaled the vapor. "My favorite." He carefully took a sip. "Do you ever feel burned out?"

"Not yet. When I feel getting close, I just take vacation and leave town."

"Leaving town sounds great, especially with all the overtime I've been working."

The men talked for a while and finished their tea.

"Are you ready to see the newest arrival?" Ralf asked.

"As I ever will be," the detective replied and followed his friend to the closet.

Giving him a green winter coat, Ralf said, "You know the routine."

Dieter Marro put the coat on. "Still as cold as Antarctica in there, huh?"

"Yep, and just like the whales down in Antarctica," his friend said, patting himself on the belly, "I've got my blubber."

The men grinned and walked through an automatic door. Four meters by four meters, the black preparation room offered limited space. Gray and black rubber boots and hooks with white and green scrubs, and a gray rubber suit aligned the wall on the left. Shelves with facemasks, goggles, boxes with white, gray, and clear rubber gloves, and a small hamper hung to his right.

Picking up a facemask, the detective gazed at the walls and flooring. "What happened to the renovation plans from a year ago?"

"It's a work in progress," Ralf replied, pointing at a blue exhaust fan in the ceiling. "They did this and the one in the break room about a week ago."

"About time they replaced those squeaky old things." The detective sniffed the air. "Yep, I definitely can tell the difference."

The men put protective face gear on and went into the processing room.

Burgundy paint coated the walls and flooring. One two-sided sink, five covered gurneys, four tall metal cabinets, and three rectangular metal tables with knives, scissors, needles, tubes, bowls, scales, sawing and dissecting equipment filled the room.

"I do have to warn you," his friend said and pulled a pair of white latex gloves from his left pocket. As his fingers filled the form-fitting cavities, the gloves squeaked like a pair of balloons. "In my twenty-one-year career, I've never seen such a maltreated corpse. My worst autopsy doesn't even come close."

Dieter Marro followed Ralf to the fifth gurney. His friend's statement bothered him. Numerous past case scenarios went through his head.

"If you need a break, let me know," Ralf said and lowered

the white cover to the girl's chin.

Nodding, the detective studied Manya's colorless face. Her eyes were closed. High cheekbones, wavy auburn hair, and narrow lips closely resembled Rosemary Mallwitz. This was undoubtedly her daughter. She looked so innocent, so pure…half woman, half child. He wanted to caress the girl's hair but held himself back. Ralf pulled the sheet to the collarbones.

"Goodness, gracious!" Dieter Marro exclaimed.

The dismembered head and bruised neck almost made him gag. His heart fluttered. Pointing at Manya's throat, he exclaimed, "Man, those marks are wide! What…about five centimeters?"

"Correct."

"I hope this is her cause of death in lieu of the dismemberment."

"It is; asphyxiation due to strangulation."

The detective wiped his forehead. "What object could possibly create such markings?"

"Scrapings from under her fingernails pointed to a black leather belt."

"Would that even fit through regular loops?"

"I'd say 'no,' but don't take my word for it. Ready for more?" The examiner lowered the sheet to the girl's waist. Upper and lower arms and hands were in single pieces. Blood concealed each wound. Lacerations and bruises of different shapes and sizes covered the girl's wrists and torso.

As if strangulation wasn't bad enough, Dieter Marro thought and shook his head. "Why?"

"We probably will never have that answer."

The detective pointed at the girl's wrists. "Did he…?"

"Yes, he held her down and at some point even tied her up. But she was a fighter and, at the minimum, scratched the heck out of him. I recovered plenty of skin and blood samples from her nails."

Sighing, Dieter Marro said, "Too bad that we can only determine blood types at this time."

Ralf raised his right index finger and shook it while talking, "One of these days, DNA will be utilized beyond our wildest imagination."

"That would be a highlight in my career. What about sexual activity?"

The examiner pulled the sheet to Manya's ankles.

Momentarily looking away, Dieter Marro said, "Oh my goodness! How in the world…?" A 'maltreated corpse' is an understatement, he thought. His nightmares and cases were breezes compared to this.

"Do you need a moment?" Ralf asked.

"No, go ahead. I'm all right."

His friend turned the girl's left thigh outward exposing several cuts and marks.

"Man!" the detective shouted. "Does this ever end?"

"You've seen nothing so far."

Widening his eyes, Dieter Marro asked, "It gets worse?"

"Look at her skin around the genital area."

"Are those finger imprints?"

"Yep, and to answer your other question: the abrasions, discolorations, and finger imprints definitely indicate repeated nonconsensual sexual activity."

"That animal." Dieter Marro said, shivering. "Doesn't this bother you? Where I'm all shaken up, you seem as calm as can be."

"Of course it bothers me…but after all these years, you get used to the blood, bruises, cuts, and everything else that comes with bodies. I only hope that this is a single case. A prematurely ended life is bad enough…but imagine two or three of these."

"I prefer not to." The detective scratched his neck. "Anything else I need to know?"

"As you can see, Ms. Mallwitz had no signs of deterioration or decomposition. I concluded that the perpetrator must have stored her in some kind of locker around sub-zero temperatures. The way he cut her up, she could have been anywhere."

"A household deep-freezer?"

"Possibly."

"I got it!" Dieter Marro exclaimed. "The killer wanted to throw us off with time of death…a fruitless attempt to establish a false alibi and sense of security and control."

Ralf glanced at Manya's remains. "He probably also waited for the right moment to dump her at the ash deposit site."

"This whole case stinks. I knew it the moment Lydia told me about the girl's disappearance." Putting his hands into his pockets, he asked, "Do you have any good news for me?"

"In matter of fact, I do. When I combed the girl's hair, I found three substances."

"Is the lab work done?"

"Naturally; freshwater eel scales, a black German shepherd nail bed, and a light trace of resin."

"Resin? What's that?"

"Ever climbed trees?"

"Yes."

"It's that clear-milky pine substance, that pretty much sticks to anything: bark, branches, cones, clothing, or skin. A real pain to get off."

Bobbing his head, Dieter Marro said, "I know exactly what you're talking about. I climbed a spruce once when I was ten. To this day, I remember my mother's anger and shouting because I ruined my newest outfit."

Ralf glanced at the other gurneys.

"I better get moving," the detective said. "You seem to have a good-sized workload."

His friend shrugged his shoulders. "My bodies are not going anywhere, and five more or less minutes do not make much of a difference." He pointed at a small birthmark under Manya's left arm. "See this spot?"

The detective nodded.

"That little mark made the big difference in the

identification."

"What about the analyses of the medical and dental records?"

The examiner covered the girl's remains. "Already completed, thanks to Captain Clark who put highest priority on the case. The girl's identity has been a hundred percent confirmed." Ralf activated the door.

Throwing his facemask and goggles into the hamper, Dieter Marro followed his friend to the break room. He hung the coat in the closet and sat on the couch.

After discarding his gloves, Ralf pulled his facemask and goggles down. "Would you like some coffee since I'm out of tea?"

"I'm okay for now." Staring at the floor, the detective said, "One thing is clear: Manya never deserved to die like this. Despite her parents' divorce, she was an affectionate, smart, and uplifting young woman. She was very well liked. The family was close-knit: mother, daughter, and son."

"How do you know so much personal information?"

"Ever since the girl disappeared, I kept in touch with her mother," Dieter Marro replied.

"She always talked about her children. Sadly, her life will never be the same after today."

"Will you be notifying her?"

"Yes. She actually called me two days ago and wanted to meet for dinner tonight. Dinner is still on, but she has no idea what's coming down."

"Why doesn't the sheriff notify her?"

"Because my boss ordered me to do so. Perhaps, he thought that she might be more comfortable to hear the news from me in lieu of some stranger."

"Possibly."

"You know, it's emotional and nerve-racking enough to solve cases and work with disturbed families," the detective said. "But telling a loving mother that her child is gone? That's the worst news anybody could ever give. She'll probably throw me out and never speak to me again."

"I highly doubt that."

"You'd be amazed what some people do in denial or after a person's death." He sighed. "Ever since Lieutenant Smirnov gave the order to notify her, my stomach has been a knot. And it seems to get tighter by the hour, especially now since I've seen Manya's remains. What am I going to do?"

"Ease up and use your own experience as guidance," Ralf said. "Personally, I think you worry about nothing. She invited you over which tells me that you're already a friend of the family."

"You're probably right."

The examiner checked his watch. "Whoa! I better get back to work, or my boss will turn me into a corpse."

"Shall we do lunch tomorrow?"

"Sure…is noon okay?"

"Noon it will be, my friend," Dieter Marro said and departed.

17

Startled, Rosemary sat up. Daydreaming about her daughter, she had fallen asleep. She looked at the living clock. It was almost six. Her left ear throbbed from pressing against the armrest of the couch. Discovering the pillow near her feet, she picked it up and placed it next to the other pillow on the couch. A whiff of basil reminded her of the roast in the oven. The woman glided into her slippers and headed to the kitchen. As she set the table and dished up the food, the bell rang.

Walking into the corridor, Rosemary shouted, "I'll be there in a minute!" She stopped at the mirror, straightened her hair with her fingertips, and pulled on the hem of her blouse to remove some wrinkles. Opening the door, she said, "Hello, Detective Marro."

"Good evening, Ms. Mallwitz," Dieter Marro greeted. He pointed at the accompanying men in uniform. "Officer Tim Karls…Officer Ron Braun."

She looked from one person to another and frowned. "I thought the detective and I were having dinner. What's going on? Michael's not in trouble, is he?"

"Our visit has nothing to do with your son," Dieter Marro calmly replied.

"Come in." Rosemary showed the men into the kitchen. "Have a seat. Give me a moment, so I can add more coal to the oven. I dozed off and got so busy afterwards that I haven't had a chance." She left. The men heard her go down some steps.

"Wow," the detective whispered, staring at the table. A glazed chocolate cake and steamy bowls with potatoes, green beans, meat, and gravy surrounded two sets of gold-rimmed plates with silverware. The aroma made his stomach growl.

She returned. "I wish I had known; I would have prepared more food."

"No need to worry," Dieter Marro said. "Due to another

appointment, we'll be unable to stay anyway." He cleared his throat. "Please sit down."

She nervously scratched her right lower arm and sat across from the detective.

"We have located your daughter."

Rosemary's face lit up. "You found Manya? Is she all right? When can I see her?"

Dieter Marro slowly shook his head. "I'm sorry."

"No!" she shouted and covered her face with her hands. "No, no, no! Can't be! This got to be some kind of mix-up."

The detective approached and put his left hand on her right shoulder. "Manya's birthmark and her medical and dental records confirmed identity."

"Why? Why is this happening? My daughter never hurt a soul!" Shivering, the woman grabbed his hand on her shoulder and wept. "I…I…I can't accept that. What am I going to do? How am I supposed to go on without Manya?"

Dieter Marro retrieved a handkerchief from his chest pocket and placed it into her palm. "I asked myself the same questions seventeen years ago and know exactly how you feel. I'd give anything to spare you from this."

Rosemary momentarily held her breath and looked down. Glancing at Ron Braun, the detective tilted his head toward the door. The officers left.

"Just like me, you have but one choice: to move on," Dieter Marro said. Gently stroking her right shoulder, he paused. "When my wife and daughter died, I had nothing left. I dedicated my life to the job. But you-you still have Michael. You've got to give your best in raising that precious child and turn him into the fine young man he ought to be.

"During our monthly conversations, I've seen your strength, perseverance, and love. I'd like to see you keep them up. Don't stop now. The power lies within you. I know you can do it!"

Rosemary stopped crying, dried her face, and rose. "Right now I really don't know what to think or do. All I know is that

Michael will be home in about an hour. I would like some time to absorb this and figure out how to tell him before he walks through the door. Could you please leave?"

"Sure, I understand," Dieter Marro said and joined the officers in the hallway. She walked the men out. The detective shook her hand and squeezed it. "If you ever need a shoulder to cry on or somebody to talk to, I'm only a phone call away."

"Thank you."

Dieter Marro followed the officers down the steps and turned around. "Think of it like this: if Manya were to look down from Heaven, what would she think? What would she want you to do?"

Rosemary thought for a moment. "She would want me to stay strong and take care of Michael."

"Then that's what you should do."

"Can you give me any details on how my daughter died?"

"I'm afraid I can't," the detective said and joined Officer Karls and Officer Braun in the unmarked police car. The men took off. Tears filling her eyes, she closed the door.

18

Dieter Marro parked his car. Passing a bricklayer with a trowel and a mortar-filled bucket, he thought about the above-freezing temperatures. That bricklayer better hurry; winter can be very unpredictable.

He entered the rectangular stucco building. The ceiling was so high; he could have stacked seven cars on top of another, still giving him enough room to crawl. Dozens of people rushed back and forth, passing him left and right in no orderly fashion. He smelled cigarettes. A far train whistled.

To his left, a crowd studied two glass boxes with printouts. Those must be the departure and arrival cases he was talking about, the detective thought and walked by. Straight ahead, he could see several platforms through a large window. A train pulled in.

"The E35 to Leipzig has a half hour delay," a male voice announced through a speaker.

"Excuse me!" a young woman shouted from behind.

The detective turned around. Discovering a brunette with a stroller, he stepped aside. Grim-faced, the lady quickly passed.

His eyes wandered from the hall clock to his watch. It was 9:37. He frowned. "That's just wonderful, I'm seven minutes late. I hope he's still waiting." He saw a line of people leading to a white-tinted window with an oval hole in the center. This must be the ticket counter, he thought and scratched his cheek.

Now-where is he?

Searching the immediate area, he located a short strawberry-blond man on a bench. The man wore a black leather jacket and blue jeans just like he said. When their eyes met, Dieter Marro bobbed his head. The stranger returned his gesture. Pointing his right thumb at the exit, the detective left.

Outside, Dieter Marro introduced himself. They exchanged handshakes.

"Maik Dahls," the stranger said. "Please call me Maik."

"Thanks for meeting me on such short notice."

"Any time. I was surprised to get a phone call from a detective. I've led a pretty decent and honest life and have never had any encounters with the police. When you mentioned you needed information on one of my members, I was so relieved."

A conductor's whistle set a train into motion. Cars rattled. People walked by; some chatted, some held hands. A child screamed.

Dieter Marro gazed at the bricklayer who meticulously patched hole after hole in the siding. "Can we by chance go somewhere less busy and more quiet?"

"Sure, I know of a perfect place right across the street," Maik Dahls said and pointed at a white house with a small sign above the entrance. "The Train Station Café."

"The structure looks more like a residential home."

"It originally was but they remodeled." The men crossed the street and went inside.

Scenic and locomotive pictures decorated beige walls. The aroma of coffee hung in the air. Each table was covered with white cloth, topped by a glass vase with purple flowers.

"It's cozy in here…but there are no customers?" Dieter Marro thought aloud.

"They'll be trickling in and out until lunch time. We just missed the morning rush."

The detective followed Maik Dahls to a small window table. Sitting down, he discovered a blonde in a black skirt and white blouse leaving the bathroom. She held a frilled white apron in her left hand. Their eyes met. She tied the apron around her waist and approached.

"Hello," the woman said overly friendly. "What can I get for you?"

"Do you have peppermint tea?" Dieter Marro asked.

"We do."

"I would like a cup of that and a salami roll, please."

The strawberry-blond man winked at the waitress. "And the usual for me."

"Allrighty then," the waitress said and smiled. Crossing the room, she disappeared behind a steel door.

"Do you come here often?" the detective inquired.

"I drop in twice a week and have tried all breakfast items. Everything's fresh, reasonable, and scrumptious. Service is excellent."

The waitress reappeared with a large empty tray. Clearing cups, plates, silverware, and small porcelain teapots from several tables, she occasionally glanced over.

Maik Dahls unzipped his jacket halfway. He pulled out a stapled stack of papers and handed it to the detective. "Here's the angler list that you requested. Luckily, we still had our files from thirty years ago."

Raising his eyebrows, the detective asked, "How many names do you have?"

"About a thousand."

"A thousand?" Dieter Marro couldn't believe his ears. Never did he suspect that an angler club could have that many members. "Are all active?"

"No, some are active, some inactive, others are deceased, or have moved out of state." Maik Dahls wrinkled his forehead. "Isn't that what you requested?"

"It is. I just didn't expect that many members." Glancing over the top page, the detective thought, Looks like I'll be spending the rest of the year going through that. He noticed that each person had some strange letter combination.

"My secretary put status codes after each name and deciphered them on the back."

Turning the list over, Dieter Marro nodded. "I was wondering about that." He put the stack of papers into his briefcase.

Maik Dahls unzipped the rest of his jacket. "Is there anything else I can help you with?"

"I do have a few questions."

"Go ahead."

The waitress returned with the orders.

Dieter Marro carefully took a sip. "How long have you been president of the angler club?"

"About nine years."

"Quite some time. And before that?"

"Committed member for five years."

"Do you consider yourself an avid fisherman?"

"Let's see: unless I'm on vacation; I participate at all events, involve and motivate people in committees, help organize activities, give free lectures, donate money, take off work for excursions with our retirees who I also supply with bait and tackle, and explore new fishing opportunities for our members. My involvement reflects my passion. Do I consider myself an avid fisherman? You bet!"

"How did you get started?"

"My father set my path. Ever since I turned seven, he took me fishing on a regular basis. After marriage and the birth of my twin daughters, things changed. We now only visit my parents on holidays and for two weeks each summer. While my wife, children, and mother do things in town or at home, Dad and I have our time on the lake. Fishing is the most wonderful sport in the world. I never seem to get enough of it."

"I assume your father is a member as well?"

"He used to be until he and mother moved away eleven years ago. If you consider asking him for information, I don't think he can be of any help. He easily forgets things, especially names and faces."

"That bad, huh?"

"Yes, and it seems to get worse every year." He paused. Looking out of the window, Maik Dahls said, "Last summer, he asked Mom who my wife and children were."

"Wow! What about your mother?"

"She despises any killing for food and never attended

meetings or activities."

Dieter Marro ate his roll and drank some tea. "Does anybody take their dog to angler activities?"

"A lot of members do. Canines are excellent fishing buddies."

"Do you recall ever seeing a black German shepherd?"

The strawberry-blond man narrowed his eyes. "Did I hear you say black?"

"Yes."

Maik Dahls scratched the top of his head. "I know lots about fishing but almost nothing about dogs. Honestly, I thought all German shepherds were brown with a black patch on the back." He shrugged his shoulders. "I'm sorry."

"What kind of fish does the club specialize in?"

"We have no specialization."

"What about your competitions?"

"At all competitions, we go by weight, not by the type of fish we catch."

"So anybody could have freshwater eel on their pole?"

"Eel? Good luck on that one! Catching an eel between nine and one during the daytime is pretty much impossible. They only bite very early in the morning or extremely late at night."

"Do you know of somebody going after eel?"

The man shook his head.

Thinking about the long angler list, Dieter Marro was anxious to get back to his office. "Well, you've answered all the questions I had. Thank you for your time. I will call you if I need anything else."

Maik Dahls nodded. "Any time."

Finishing his tea, the detective put some change on the table and left.

19

Dieter Marro took his winter coat off and hung it up. Holding his hands over the radiator near the door, he thought about his conversation with Maik Dahls and the angler list. It had been two weeks and he barely made any progress. The immeasurable amount of folders, notes, lists, and papers on his desk made him sweat. How much time will it take to finish all his projects and cases? A year? He felt overwhelmed.

The phone rang. He picked it up. "Superintendent Dieter Marro. … Well, hi, Ms. Mallwitz. How are you? … Yes, I can stop by your house this weekend. Any preference? … He gazed at the angler list and closed his eyes. "I suppose I could do it this morning. … Okay, I'll see you in a bit." He hung up.

Months had passed since he told her that her daughter was gone. He had been wondering how she was doing. Rosemary insisted on meeting him at earliest convenience. What could be so important? Did an inside source give her details about the case? Lydia? No, she had always been reliable. He was curious and could hardly wait to find out. But the idea of getting back into the cold gave him the chills. Last week's freezing rain… this week's snow…and now the predicted temperature drop? How much longer will his car hold up after eighteen years? The heater already had a mind of its own. What will scream for independence next? The transmission? He put on his coat and walked out. An hour of driving passed.

Pulling in front of Rosemary's house, he still hadn't come up with a plausible answer on why she wanted to meet him. He rang the bell.

She answered the door, wearing a red turtleneck and blue twill pants. Despite the perfect makeup, her high cheekbones seemed to be more protruding than ever. He inspected her waist. It was, at the minimum, five centimeters thinner. Rosemary looked rested. "Please come in," she said.

The detective stomped and rubbed his boots on the doormat. "My goodness, this white stuff sticks to my soles like honey. If your sidewalk wasn't shoveled, I'd probably be a meter taller by now." The woman looked at his boots and faintly smiled. She rubbed her upper arms. "I'm sorry for bringing all this cold air in," he said and stepped inside.

"It's all right; the house warms up quickly." She closed the door. "May I have your coat?"

"Sure. Thank you."

She draped his garment over a wooden hanger and hooked it into the clothing rack. "I know it's getting closer to lunch time, but I was just getting ready to make me a jelly sandwich. Have you had anything to eat lately?"

Her thoughtfulness confirmed Ralf's evaluation: he already was a friend of the family. "Yes, I had a salami sandwich," he said.

"How about some tea?"

"I'd like that. My heater acted up most of the way over here, barely producing any warmth." He shivered. "I'm so froze."

Giving it some thought, she asked, "Didn't they say it was supposed to be minus fifteen degrees?"

"Something like that."

"Pretty cold." Rosemary retrieved a small object from the top shelf of the wardrobe rack and handed it to him. "Before I forget…."

"My handkerchief! Thank you. I forgot all about it." He looked the item over. "So neatly folded and ironed, it looks like you never even used it."

She faintly smiled. "Go ahead and have a seat in the living room. You may use the blanket to warm up a little. I'll be right in."

"Do you need any help?"

"I think I can handle it. Thank you, though."

Moments later she returned with an oval wicker tray. Sitting on the couch, he had covered himself with the blanket from the chest down. She distributed the dishes and tea and sat in the armchair across from him. "I hope this visit doesn't interfere too much with your schedule?"

"I've got the rest of the weekend for overtime. Besides, a little break once in a while will do me some good. Plus…" He held his handkerchief up. "I'm happy to have my hanky back."

A grin crossed her face. With a relaxed tone, she asked, "How much have you been working, if I may ask?"

"Twelve to sixteen-hour shifts for the past two weeks."

"Twelve to sixteen hours a day?" Rosemary wrinkled her forehead.

"Yep; I eat, I sleep, and I go to work. That's pretty much it."

"Your dedication is astounding. Is it Manya's case you're working on?"

The detective debated whether to disclose that information or not. He decided to keep the information to himself.

"The reason I'm asking is because I haven't heard from you or anybody else about when to expect Manya's remains. She needs to have a proper funeral. Wouldn't you agree?"

"I certainly agree," Dieter Marro said and took a sip. "However, difficult circumstances keep us from finalization. Please understand and bear with us. I'll let you know when we're getting close, okay?"

"All right."

"Anyway, I was glad to hear from you. How have you been?"

Rosemary finished her sandwich and drank some tea. "Hanging in there, I guess. I pretty much keep myself occupied between Michael, work, the house, and my hobbies. I've done more knitting and crafting in the past few weeks than I did all last year. I'm almost finished with my latest project. Would you like to see?"

"Sure."

Rosemary walked to the side of the couch, picked up a round wicker basket, and placed it next to the detective. She removed a pink garment and spread it on the table. "I still have to sow the seams but otherwise the sweater is done."

"You made that?"

"Yes, I finished knitting last night. Why?"

He touched the garment. "It's so soft and even. I bet the most advanced machine couldn't align the rows as perfectly as you do. Was it hard?"

"Not at all. Knitting comes very easy to me." She stowed the item and carried the basket to its original spot. "The sweater actually symbolizes a turning point."

"How so?"

"I remembered our last conversation when I started knitting it. From that on, I followed your advice and dedicated myself more to Michael than ever. I assist with school projects and homework, am a chaperon at all class excursions and trips, fully utilize my vacation time, and attend all soccer practices and tournaments. I even learned how to kick the ball around at home." The woman momentarily paused and smiled. "Our neighbors had quite a few unexpected visits though."

"I'd consider that normal. Any broken windows?"

"No. Thankfully my neighbors' houses are further in the back."

"I'm proud of you," he said and glanced at the wall behind her. Pointing at a photo, he asked, "You and Michael went to Museums Island?"

She nodded. "Even though it takes hours to get there, Berlin was on our agenda several times during break. In addition to the Pergamon Museum, we visited the Historical Museum, saw Swan Lake at the State Opera, swam in the famous indoor wave pool, took a steamboat ride, and had a picnic next to the Soviet Soldier Memorial."

"How is Michael doing?"

"He mopes, is very clingy, and, except for the extra-curricular activities, prefers to stay at home. His grades go up and down. But what concerns me the most is that two weeks have passed since he last played with his close friend George."

"He'll come around," the detective said.

"I hope so. His sadness tears me up. Every night, I sit on his bed and talk to him. Sometimes I hold his hand and sometimes I caress his hair, before tucking him in. Many mornings, I wake up with Michael all curled up next to me."

Dieter Marro drank some tea. "Is he in his room?"

"No, he's spending the weekend with his aunt and uncle. But I didn't contact you to tell you all this; I called because I'd like to ask you for a favor."

"What kind of favor?"

She thought about the lowering temperature and the improperly working heater in the detective's car and deemed them as minor obstacles. Looking him straight into the eyes, she said, "Please take me to the place where Manya was found."

He raised his brows. "You want me to do what?"

"I'd like you to take me to the area where my daughter was found."

Her request stunned him. He thought of the promotion his boss had promised him. "I don't know if that is such a good idea."

"I had plenty of time to think about it and made up my mind."

"No, I understand and would love to take you. It's just that my job prohibits the disclosure of any information."

Rosemary opened a table drawer and removed a tightly knitted white cross. She kissed the palm-sized object and gently glided her fingers over it. "I didn't tell you; but before I started that pink sweater, I made this in remembrance of Manya. I chose white because it's the color of innocence. Manya was virtuous and blameless and the best daughter a mother could ever have." She slowly approached. "A friend starched and lacquered the cross to enhance durability in the elements. I now would like to give it a permanent place."

"I…I just don't know."

Rosemary, determined, placed the cross into his right palm.

"From a mother to a father…please, I'm begging you, fastening the cross at the site will give me peace and consolation. Put yourself into my position and feel what I feel. What is your heart telling you to do?"

Her clever approach left him speechless. He stared at the object. All the cases he had worked on, nobody had ever been so bold and requested anything like this. What if somebody sees them? Should he risk the only future he has?

Rosemary left. Moments later she returned. Standing in the door, she held a white winter coat toward him. "With all the snow, this is the best camouflage you could ask for," she said and lowered her arms. "The last thing on my mind is getting you in trouble, especially since you and Lydia have helped my friends and family so much."

"All right, all right," he said, defensively raising his left hand. "I'll do it…but please, no more requests like this."

"I'll do my best to restrain myself," she said, putting the coat away. She returned and reached for the porcelain teapot on the table. "More tea?"

Looking outside, Dieter Marro noticed that it was snowing lightly. "We better head out. It's a long drive and the storm is supposed to get worse as the temperature drops. I don't want to take any chances in getting stuck and being seen at or near the site." He returned the cross. "You better hold onto that before I lose it."

"Okay."

The detective followed Rosemary into the hallway. Helping her with the coat, he asked, "Sure you up to this?"

"Yes." She stuffed the cross into her purse and put her boots, hat, and mittens on. "I'm ready."

After he bundled up, they went outside. It had stopped snowing. He quickly shoveled the sidewalk before escorting her to the car. Starting the vehicle, he turned the heater on. It worked perfectly. After a slow two-hour drive, he parked the car near the entrance of the ash deposit site.

"Here?" Rosemary asked, staring at the closed gate.

"You requested to see the place where Manya was found; this is it."

"Why would she be here? Manya went to get rolls. This is far off from Mark's town. And…what is this place anyway? All I see is forest, a three-meter fence with a gate, and strange piles covered with snow."

"It's an ash deposit site for a local company." He placed his right hand on her left shoulder. "Look, if you're uncomfortable, I'd be happy to turn around and forget that we ever came here."

Rosemary shook her head and removed her mittens. Taking the cross and a short wire from her purse, she said, "I came here with a purpose and wont leave until that is fulfilled. Could you please give me a few moments?"

"Sure."

She got out of the car. Holding the cross near her heart, she observed the fence and nearby trees. Which way should I go, she thought, turning her head back and forth. She went east since there were fewer branches in the path. The sky grew dark. A strong wind picked up, tugging on her coat and howling through the nearby forest. Trees cracked.

Rosemary walked several minutes before stopping. She kissed the cross and fastened it to the fence. Gazing at her accomplishment, she nodded, satisfied. Her hat blew off. She picked it up and hurried to the car.

"You're all right?" the detective asked as she sank into the passenger seat. He noticed several streaks under her eyes. Rosemary bobbed her head. Staring at the windshield, she wiped her face with a handkerchief. It snowed again. Large snowflakes hit the tempered glass and shrank into lumps of ice water.

Dieter Marro activated the windshield wipers, put the car into gear, and took off. He wondered if she suspected anything. If she only knew the truth….

The car unexpectedly slid sideways. Counter-steering, he straightened the vehicle. "Everything's under control."

She didn't make a sound and only stared out of the passenger window.

The detective imagined her crying. He thought about the loss of his own child. His heart sank with sorrow and pain.

Upon arrival, Dieter Marro followed Rosemary into the house. "I'll make you some tea," he said and went into the kitchen. After taking her boots, mittens, hat, and coat off, she sat on the living room couch. The teakettle whistled.

Dieter Marro entered with a tray. He poured tea into a cup and placed it in front of her. "I should get going since you probably want some time to yourself."

"No, please stay. I really would like some company right now."

He gave it some thought. "All right. I'll stay."

She finished her tea.

"I'll take care of that," the detective said, putting her cup and the dishes from before on the tray. Like a waiter, he placed the tray on his right shoulder and carried it into the kitchen.

Through the open door, Rosemary was able to hear him fill the sink with water. Feeling at ease, she leaned back, and supported her head with a couch pillow. She fell asleep.

Manya repeatedly rode her new bike up and down the block. As if she had imaginary springs, the girl bounced her body off the saddle. Grinning, Manya waved each time she passed the gate.

Rosemary woke up. In a daze, she checked her surroundings. She recognized her living room. Dieter Marro sat under the lit standing lamp and read one of Michael's soccer brochures. It was pitch-black outside. The detective put the magazine down and smiled. "Feeling okay?"

"Yes," she replied and wondered how that man got into her house. As grogginess faded, she remembered. Straightening her hair with her fingertips, she said, "I dreamed about Manya's last birthday. She was so happy."

He smiled. "I wish I could have been there."

The kitchen timer went off. Dieter Marro rose. "If you'd excuse me, I better take the meatloaf out of the oven." He left.

After dinner, Rosemary moved closer. She unexpectedly rested her hand on his lower arm. "I appreciate everything you've done for me and my family. However, something has been bothering me ever since we left the ash deposit site. I want you to be straightforward: was Manya murdered?"

This woman was just full of surprises. What am I going to do? He dreaded to think of what she might ask for next. His parents had raised him with honesty, which in this instance could cost him his job or worse. Trapped, he had to make a choice… here and now. Putting his left hand on top of hers, Dieter Marro said, "Yes."

Sitting back, Rosemary covered her face and loudly exhaled.

He didn't dare to move or say anything.

She put her hands down and stared at Michael's soccer magazines on the table. "Can you tell me anything…something?"

He shook his head. "I wish I could."

"First, the police prohibits spreading the word, and now you're keeping the truth from us? This is not just a conspiracy; it's a double cover up!"

He wanted to crawl into the deepest hole on earth. The damage was done. "Between you and me, I agree with everything you say. I feel for you…but my hands are tied. You are a good mother. Please accept the circumstances for what they are. I hate to see something happening to you or Michael because you're simply not following the rules. That's all I'm going to say." With a stricter tone, he asked, "Do we have an understanding?"

At first, she hesitated…then she nodded.

The rest of the evening they talked about the children, themselves, and life in general. At departure around midnight, Dieter Marro had an idea. "How about having a phone installed?"

Rosemary thought about Michael. When away from home, he would always be able to get a hold of her. "I love the idea," she said. "However, I've heard of somebody who's got heart problems and has been waiting for a phone for at least nineteen years. Nobody in this household has any medical condition. Why would they give us a phone or even consider adding us to their list?"

"Forget the medical necessity! Your daughter's disappearance is far more serious, don't you agree? And that's how I'm going to push it. If my idea falls through, I'll figure out something else. I promise you'll have a phone by the end of next week."

"Michael and I would appreciate that." She opened the door for him. It quit snowing. Dieter Marro stepped outside. "Oh, detective," Rosemary said.

Turning around, he asked, "Yes?"

She extended her hand. "Please call me Rosemary."

"You may call me Dieter." They shook hands.

Suddenly hugging him, she said, "Thank you for everything."

"You're welcome. I'll see you around." He walked to his car and took off.

20

The last snow had just melted, leaving the ground soft and moist. It was chilly. Dieter Marro stopped at the two-story yellow brick house and got out of the car. Stunned, he halted his step. Never had he seen such architecture and creativity on a residential home. In addition to encasing all windows, green fifteen-centimeter beams interchanged with bricks in a horizontal, vertical, and diagonal pattern. Three carved square pillars of the same color and width held a small tar roof over two wooden doors with lace curtains. Carved brackets supported each pillar on top. Somebody had painted a white square with a black '7' on the center pillar. Two separate rows of red bricks trimmed the house one meter from the ground. Differing thickness and slight bowing of the pickets reflected genuine craftsmanship of a fence builder. Even without the beams and bricks, the house would have attracted anyone's attention due to a preserved head of a three-point buck between the second-story windows.

The detective noticed a gray-haired woman watching from the right first-floor window. He passed through the gate. It had been months since he started tackling the angler list. So many visits, so many phone calls, and nothing but dead-ends. Did the perpetrator just snap his fingers and hypnotize everybody, erasing all memories? Dieter Marro was so desperate; he wanted to scream. This was his last address…his last chance.

At the doors, he straightened his brown suit and looked at his feet. He despised wearing khaki shoes on moist grounds but had no choice since his black pair fell apart and his brown shoes were getting repaired at the shoemaker. To his delight, he found no speck of dirt on the leather. He rang the bell and waited. His feet tingled.

A man in his seventies opened the door wearing dress pants and a knit sweater. "Good evening, can I help you?"

"I'm Superintendent Dieter Marro with the Halle police

department," the detective said and showed his identification. "I'd like to speak with Mr. and Mrs. Klaus Hof. I sent them a letter a few days ago that I would be visiting today."

The older man stroked his beard and inspected the badge. "I'm Klaus Hof. I apologize for the distrust. Letter or no letter, ever since somebody robbed us two years ago, we use extreme caution around strangers."

"I understand."

"Please come in."

Dieter Marro stepped inside. The house smelled like beeswax and cinnamon. Sconces with candles and dried flowers hung on the corridor walls. Preserved laurel framed the oblong hallway mirror and wall-mounted wooden wardrobe rack. "If you'd please follow me," the older man said, taking the detective to the room at the end of the corridor.

Amidst a preserved squirrel, hedgehog, fox pup, and turtle, assorted books filled several shelves and cabinets. A large picture of a deer family in the forest hung on the wall across from the door. In the center, a rectangular table was set for three. Pointing at one of the four armchairs, Klaus Hof said, "Have a seat. This is our study. Gorki, Fontane, London…nothing is more relaxing than a good book in your hand and a cup of coffee."

A short woman in a plaid dress appeared in the doorway. Dieter Marro recognized the lady from the window.

"My wife Maria," Klaus Hof said.

Exchanging handshakes, she asked, "Coffee or tea, detective?"

"Tea, please."

"Would you like cream or sugar?"

"No, thank you," Dieter Marro said, getting a pen and notebook from his briefcase. "I like my tea plain."

Maria Hof left. The older man sat across from him. "We were just getting ready to have dinner…hope you brought your appetite."

Mrs. Hof returned with a teapot and egg and liverwurst

sandwiches. After distributing the tea, she looked at Dieter Marro. "Please, help yourself."

"Detective," Klaus Hof said and picked a liverwurst sandwich. "Your letter was very vague. Is your visit in regards to the robbery?"

"No, I'm actually working on something different and need information on a fishing buddy."

"An angler from the club?" The older man exchanged looks with his wife. "How interesting. What's the angler's name?"

"I was hoping that you could help me with that."

"Easier said than done. You're talking about an awful long time frame with many ever-changing faces."

Dieter Marro twisted the tip of his pen and opened his notebook. "You were a member of the club for twelve years, correct?"

"Yes, I joined after I took an early retirement from my forestry job. However, I also visited for about three years prior to that."

The detective took some notes. "Any particular reason why you hesitated joining?"

"I'm a man of honor. Before I make a commitment, I always test the waters."

Helping herself to an egg sandwich, Maria Hof said, "I bear witness to that. It took him two years before he asked Father for my hand, and, believe it or not, he is still loving, devoted, and supportive after fifty-two years as he was the day we got married." She reached for the teapot. "More tea, anybody?"

"No thank you, dear," her husband replied and winked at her.

Dieter Marro raised his cup and saucer toward the woman. "Please." She refilled his cup. The detective carefully took a sip. "Now, Mr. and Mrs. Hof, during those years as members or visitors were you ever absent for a long period of time?"

"Only once when I had my bypass surgery," Klaus Hof replied.

"When was that?"

"About thirteen years ago in November."

"How long were you gone?" the detective inquired, taking a liverwurst sandwich from the plate.

"Five months."

"Quite some time."

"When I initially went in for chest pain, the doctor also discovered that I had diabetes. It took me all those months to recover and find a newer and healthier lifestyle I was comfortable with." Dieter Marro scribbled something into his notebook.

"Do you think our absence might have had an impact on your case?" Maria Hof asked.

"I wouldn't worry about it," the detective said and bit into his sandwich.

The bell rang twice. Klaus Hof left. Within a minute, he returned. "Nobody there…probably just some kids playing."

Dieter Marro finished eating. "I understand that a lot of men bring their dogs fishing. Do you recall ever seeing a black German shepherd or a large dog with unusual behavior like aggression?"

The older man lowered his head. "It's very typical to have a bark here or there at activities. But anything out of the ordinary…not that I remember."

"Mrs. Hof?"

"I do recall a strange encounter at one of the first fishing competitions we attended," she said.

"So around fifteen or sixteen years ago?" the detective inquired.

"Something like that."

"Where was the competition at?"

"Near Boizenburg at the upper Elbe River."

"Was it a black German shepherd?"

"I'm a cat person and have never had interest in canines or their breeds. All I remember is that the dog was big and black. The animal growled, jumped, and even tried to nip us when we passed. However, the behavior was nothing compared to the dog's condition and treatment."

Frowning, Dieter Marro asked, "What do you mean by that?"

"Each time the dog jumped, the steel collar tightened, making the animal gasp for air. The fur was clumped into fist-sized balls. And boy, was the dog skinny! The rib cage and hip bones protruded as if the animal hadn't been fed for weeks." She looked at her husband. "I'm surprised you don't remember any of this!"

"I'm sorry my memory is not as good as it used to be," Klaus Hof said. "That's why I keep you around."

She smiled.

The detective made several notes in his notebook. "Any specifics about the dog's owner?"

Taking a sip, she made a face as if her tea was replaced by lemon juice. "After Klaus and I walked by, I turned around and saw the owner ruthlessly kick the animal in the side. The dog squealed in pain."

"You should have told me," her husband said. "I would have set him straight."

"Set him straight? You most likely would have made things worse."

"You're probably right," he said and helped himself to an egg sandwich. "Is there anything else I might have forgotten and should know about?"

"I looked into the man's eyes and saw so much hatred and degradation, it about scared me to death." She shivered. "And it gets worse."

Her husband quit chewing. "Really?"

"You should have seen his wife."

Lowering his cup, the detective asked, "He had somebody with him?"

"Yes! She sat on a nearby rock and stared at the gleaming water."

"What did the woman look like?"

"Pretty little thing with waist-length brown hair and light-complected skin. I estimate her height at around five feet, weighing no more than forty-five kilograms. The lady barely seemed old enough to be married."

"How do you know she was married?" Klaus Hof inquired.

"I think I saw a gold band on her ring finger. But I'm not a hundred percent sure."

Flipping the page in his notebook, the detective asked, "What did she wear?"

"A light-colored long-sleeved blouse and dark pants. Such a shame that she put up with him." Maria Hof shook her head. "I just don't understand."

"Did you notice anything else?"

She gave it some thought. "Oh, one time the woman pushed a strand of hair from her face. Her sleeve slid to her elbow. The arm was covered with large dark spots."

Dieter Marro stopped writing and looked up. "You mean bruises?"

Maria Hof nodded. "The woman quickly lowered her hand and pulled her sleeve down. But the guy already noticed. He screamed at her like there was no tomorrow. I could tell she held her tears back. My heart yearned to comfort her but I didn't. I was just too scared. Who knows…he probably would have chopped our heads off!"

Klaus Hof curled his left hand into a fist. "A man should never hurt a woman! If I ever get my hands on that bastard, I'd…"

"You would do exactly nothing!" his wife cut him off. "You need to think of your health; getting upset will only give you high blood pressure and another heart attack. In addition, he could put you in jail!"

"All right."

"This couple gets more interesting by the minute," the detective said and made several notations. "Did you ever get his or her name?"

"We talked to Manfred about the encounter. He thought his first name started with an 'A' but he wasn't for certain. And that's as far as we got. I don't know how important this might be, but the couple never returned to any other activity from the club."

"What did the man look like?"

She took a sip. "He had a tanned face as if he spends a great deal outside. His hair was brown, a little lighter than hers, and very short."

"How short?"

"About three centimeters or so."

"What about his age and build?"

Maria Hof picked up the last sandwich and put it on her plate. "He couldn't have been older than forty and had a similar statue like my husband: about two meters and a hundred twenty kilograms. Coming to think of it: I believe the guy worked for the force."

"The Army?"

"No," she said, shaking her head. "Police."

Dieter Marro wrinkled his forehead. "An officer of the law?"

"At least that's what Manfred said."

"What is Manfred's last name?"

"Bartels." Gazing at the egg sandwich on her plate, she paused.

Klaus Hof softly stroked his wife's left hand on the armrest. "Manfred was a close family friend for over forty years. He was the one who actually invited us to the club."

The detective retrieved the angler list from his briefcase and browsed through the pages. "Here he is," he said and stared at the abbreviated status. No wonder he didn't remember visiting with him.

"After a seven-month battle, Manfred passed away of pancreatic cancer last summer," Maria Hof said. "It was very hard on all of us."

"I'm sorry for your loss. You have my deepest sympathy." Placing the list, notebook, and pen into his briefcase, Dieter Marro rose, "This concludes my visit. Thank you for your time, tea, and sandwiches. You've been a great help. If you remember anything else, please give me a call. Do you still have my letter?"

"We kept it in case we needed to call you to reschedule," Klaus Hof said. "With my heart history and ongoing diabetes, you never know."

The detective nodded.

Klaus and Maria Hof showed the visitor out. The sun had set. A flock of screeching birds passed, going north.

The woman put her hand on Dieter Marro's shoulder. "I realize a few years have passed, but if you find that woman, please make sure that she gets away from that monster of a husband. She doesn't deserve to live like that. Promise you'll help her?"

"You have my word."

"And…if that man has any animals, place them into a better home."

"I'll do my best, Mrs. Hof."

She put her right hand on her chest and, relieved, exhaled. "I feel so much better and hope to have made a positive impact on this world."

Klaus Hof embraced his wife and pulled her closer. He shook the detective's hand. "Best of luck on your investigation."

Dieter Marro took off.

21

Passing deciduous and pine trees, the young woman ran as fast as her legs carried. Fear widened her eyes. Branches shredded her white blouse and black pants and punctured her petite body like miniature daggers. Small twigs, pine needles, and leaves tangled in her waist-length brown hair.

"Help! Help! Somebody help me!" she screamed from the top of her lungs.

Dieter Marro saw her through a clearing and wildly moved his arms to get her attention. "Here, come over here!" he yelled. But she didn't see or hear him. He collected his strength and dashed toward her. His brown suit tore. His black shoes fell apart. Twigs whipped him everywhere, leaving thin trails of blood on exposed areas. The wounds throbbed. He repeatedly motivated himself: I can do it. She needs my help.

Closing in, he now estimated a distance of less than twenty meters. Another clearing. "Here, come over here!" he quickly shouted and waved. Again, she didn't hear or see him. His anxiety grew the closer he got…only ten more meters…nine…eight… seven…six…. Heat rose into his upper body and face. Sweat stung his eyes.

The forest's structure suddenly became different. A patch of wide tree trunks now interchanged with two-meter firs.

The woman tripped over a thick root and fell.

Dieter Marro yearned to help her up and take her away. However, as if somebody strung lead weights around his knees, his feet suddenly stopped moving. He wanted to scream 'get up and run' but his tongue was immobile. He tried to reach for her but his arms were paralyzed.

His heart ached as he helplessly watched a man with short brown hair catch up to her. The stranger's height leveled with the firs. Compared to the woman's build and age, the man in the coverall looked like a plump giant and easily could have been her father. His evil look left no doubt about him ever letting her get away.

The detective discovered something in the stranger's hands. With a tree trunk in the way, he could only see a thick black handle. What is that, he thought. As the stranger pulled a string and powered up the object, it dawned on him: it was a chainsaw. Dieter Marro held his breath.

The brunette rose to her knees. "Let me live!"

Stomping his right foot on the woman's upper spine, the stranger pushed her back down. "So, you want to live?" he asked.

She lifted her head and moaned. "Y…e…s." Moss and pine needles stuck on her blood- and dirt-smeared face.

"Then you shouldn't have shown off your bruises!"

"It was an accident!" she cried. "My hair was tickling my face. I had to push it aside."

"You ruined my reputation and destroyed our marriage. Therefore, you must die!" The stranger increased the speed of his power tool.

"Please let me live!" she begged once more, frantically wiggling her body to break free.

"I…" he said, merciless cutting her right arm off. "Don't…" the man stated as he severed her left arm. "Think…" he said, cutting her right leg off. "So," the man stated as he severed her left leg and head. Blood squirted onto to the perpetrator's face, arms, and clothing and soaked the ground.

The man with the chainsaw looked up and saw the detective. Narrowing his eyes and rising, he asked, "Wanna run and tell?"

Dieter Marro shook his head. He wanted to beg for his life but, still, no sound came out of his mouth.

Approaching, the killer grinned and moved his chainsaw up and down. The detective smelled the man's foul breath and, disgusted, turned his head. He wanted to run off but his legs were still frozen. How can I get out of this, he thought.

The stranger lifted the chainsaw to his right arm. "I…

don't…think…so…."

Dieter Marro felt the power tool dig into his flesh. Excruciating pain ran through his body, triggering severe muscle spasms. He closed his eyes. Thinking of his wife and daughter, he felt at peace …and smiled.

The chainsaw became louder and louder…when the detective suddenly woke up by the sound of his alarm. He slammed his fingers on the snooze button, shoving the round metal clock several inches backwards. The sun was rising. Birds happily announced the new day.

Pushing the covers aside, Dieter Marro sat up. His t-shirt, boxers, pillow, and bed sheet were soaked with sweat. He raised his hands above his head, touched his neck, and stuck his tongue out. "Everything in order. Thank goodness." Shaking his head and rolling his eyes, the detective jumped out of bed. He showered, ate breakfast, and went to work.

"Morning, lieutenant," he greeted his boss in the hallway and yawned.

"Man, you look like you had a sleepless night."

"I feel like a train ran over me. A train loaded with the mother of all nightmares."

"That bad, huh?"

Dieter Marro bobbed his head.

"I read your report about the latest developments," the lieutenant said. "Anything to do with that?"

"Everything! The conversation with the Hof couple must have slipped into my sub-conscience which then turned around and spun its own tale."

Two officers passed and went into the nearby break room. The aroma of coffee spread.

"We need to talk," the lieutenant said. "Follow me."

The sound of his boss's voice made him cringe. He felt like a puppy with his tail squeezed between his legs after doing something wrong. Questions raced through his mind: What if he fires me because I'm so far behind on my cases? Maybe he changed his mind about retiring. Maybe he changed his mind about my promotion? A chill went down his spine. Did they find the cross at the ash deposit site? If so, was it traced back to Rosemary? What if they put me in jail? What if they kill me?

They walked into his boss's office. The lieutenant closed the door. A framed Erich Honecker stared at him from the wall to his right. The president's eyes seemed to follow every step he took. Dieter Marro turned his head. A large new bookcase held a sorted arsenal on forensics, regulations, investigations, world history, and deaths. His throat tightened. Books on the latest subject were not aligned and appeared to stick out by one or two centimeters. He was scared for his life and so wished to have stayed at home today.

"Have a seat," his boss said and pointed at the black armchair across from his desk. "Since time is limited, I'm gonna get straight to the point: your report concerns me."

A huge weight lifted from the detective's shoulders. He was so delighted; he could have hugged the lieutenant. "As far as I know, I included everything."

"The report itself is fine, and you're doing a great job on the case. I'm just worried about what kind of person we might have on our hands. A perpetrator working for law enforcement is like a loose bullet in a shopping center at Christmas. What if he's a serial killer? The outcome could be devastating for our country and its reputation. You need to get to the bottom of this at earliest convenience."

Dieter Marro thought about his current workload. Despite the overtime, he had barely made any progress over the past few weeks. He didn't dare to think of a prioritization. Boldly, he asked, "What about the rest of my cases?"

The lieutenant leaned against his desk. "They are now Detective Winkelmann and Detective Taler's problems."

"Who's Detective Winkelmann?"

"A transfer from Cottbus. Arriving sometimes this afternoon, he will assist us until you solve the Mallwitz case."

"I see." Relief flared up. Dieter Marro loudly exhaled.

His boss gave him a list. "The reassignment of your cases. Detective Taler will stop by in about an hour to help you sort. Upon completion, he'll take his cases to his office."

"Where will Detective Winkelmann be located?"

The lieutenant pointed his thumb to his left. "He'll be in the empty office next to mine. Back to the Mallwitz case, what's your next move?"

"Identification of the suspect."

"How will you go about that?"

Staring at the bookcase, Dieter Marro said, "I will contact the national police academy in Bernau and request graduation records from nineteen forty-five through nineteen seventy-one."

"That many?"

"I'd rather have too many suspects than not enough and miss our one person of interest. He could have been younger or older than Maria Hof observed. Therefore, I thought a deviation of seven years either way should suffice. And since eighteen is the minimum age of candidates entering the academy, nineteen forty-five was a good starting point."

His boss raised his eyebrows. "I'm impressed! With your strategy, this case might be solved in a matter of days."

"Hold on. It certainly will take longer than that."

"I know. I was just kidding. Loosen up!"

The detective mischievously grinned. "Okay, just remember me when you retire next year. I want that promotion."

"We'll just have to see, don't we?" The lieutenant walked to the door. "Oh, one more thing: I'm having Detective Taler cross-reference all homicidal deaths in our country."

Pointing at the out-of-order books on the shelf, Dieter Marro asked, "From your inventory?"

"Those and others from our library in the basement," the lieutenant replied, holding the door open. "So far, nothing is like your girl's demise. You may be dismissed."

The detective rose and thought about Ralf's statement and

the morbid library. Not only was the 'Smell of Death' down there, it was the 'Basement of Death.'" "I'll draw up a facsimile for the police academy as soon as I get to my office. Will you be available to sign the request?"

His boss peeked at the clock above the door. "I'll be here for another twenty minutes before heading to a six-hour summit out of town."

"I should be able to get it done before you leave."

"I'll be expecting you," the lieutenant said, patting Dieter Marro on the shoulder. "Good work. Keep it up."

The detective walked out.

22

Dieter Marro approached the chapel. Coarse gravel crunched under his feet. Spruces, evergreens, and rhododendrons densely surrounded the round flat building, leaving one opening for the entrance. A cast-iron bell topped the center of the tiled shallow roof. Stucco columns, connected by round arches, supported an extension with clay tiles that covered brown benches and a paved ring-shaped path to the back. The landscaping and architecture offered perfect seclusion for any grieving attendee.

He entered the building and stopped. Meter-long crosses hung between film-covered arched windows on both sides. The scent of carnations and pine filled the air. Except for the main aisle and the paths to the pulpit, piano, casket, and two pew sections, pine wreaths and colorful flower arrangements covered the brick flooring. Black bows hung from the back of the seats, the piano, and the large candleholders at each side of the podium. The pews were filled with people. A woman in her sixties played soft, melancholic music on the piano.

The detective focused on the coffin. A large wreath of pine and some kind of red heart-shaped flowers with pollen stems topped the object. Lacquered mahogany stain coated the smooth even wood. Four curvy brass clips gave the casket a vintage look. Dieter Marro held his breath. It was the same style of coffin he had picked for his wife and daughter years ago. Memories popped up.

"Thank you so much for coming," Rosemary greeted to his left. She looked content. Her exquisite modern black skirt suit form-fitted her natural curves. Vanilla perfume tickled his nose.

He shook her hand. "I wanted to come sooner but I had too much going on at work."

"I understand. Please, come with me. I reserved a seat for you." She led him to the first row. Some people stared. Others whispered. The atmosphere reminded him of the day he buried his family. He felt uneasy.

Rosemary pointed at one of two adjacent seats between the aisle and Michael. "Here you go."

"Thank you."

She sat between the detective and Michael. The music stopped.

Anke walked up front, tied a white ribbon to the wreath on the casket, and hurried back to her seat.

After the pastor held his sermon, Manya's father stepped up. He introduced himself and cleared his throat. "A child is like a pound of clay that has to be formed with love, nurture, and structure to become something beautiful. The past weeks opened my eyes. I discovered that I lost my loving and nurturing touch when I accepted raises and promotions with longer hours over family. Besides my children, I also neglected my duties as a husband, not only to Elizabeth but also to Rosemary. I blame the failure of my previous marriage solely on myself. And…" he glanced at the people in the front row, "Rosemary, Elizabeth, Michael, and Amelia, I hope that you can forgive me for making those mistakes."

His eyes wandered to the casket. "I'm so privileged to have called Manya my daughter. She was a child without blemishes. Today, I would give anything to have one more minute to ask her for forgiveness, to hug and to hold her, and to whisper into her ear one last time: 'I love you.'"

He breathed in deeply and exhaled. "I can't recoup lost time of the past, but I certainly can choose the right path for the future. In hope of becoming a better father and spouse, I turned in my immediate resignation as manager this morning." Heinrich nodded at his wife, ex-wife, and son. Lowering his head, he walked back to his seat.

Tears filled Elizabeth's eyes. She tightly wrapped her arms around her daughter, kissed her on the head, and whispered into her husband's ear, "Thank you."

"Da-da-da," Amelia unexpectedly babbled aloud, turning to her father. Excited, she moved her chubby arms without coordination.

The mother gently placed a hand over the child's mouth. "Shhh."

Heinrich hugged his wife and daughter and …cried.

Silence filled the chapel. A rusty spigot squeaked somewhere outside.

Rosemary squeezed her son's hand and spoke softly, "Chin up!"

Wearing a black suit, Michael walked up front. The boy put an L-shaped cast on the coffin and went to the pulpit. Glancing at his mother, he retrieved a piece of paper from the rear pocket and unfolded it. Michael read:

"This cast represents more than just torn ligaments. It represents memories of Manya and her uplifting support and strength.

1. When I doubted dad's visit at the hospital, Manya kept up my hopes.
2. After surgery, she cheered me up and reminded me that my cast was not a disability or a permanent condition.
3. At the hospital, Manya made sure that I always had enough to drink and to eat. She also gladly pushed me around in that two-wheel contraption." He momentarily paused and smiled. *"Talking about wheelchairs…she also made sure that life was exciting and organized several races down the hallway with my roommate and another boy. When the nurses stopped us, Manya stepped up and took the fall.*
4. Believe it or not, using a long ruler, she even scratched my foot twice when I had tickle attacks under my cast.
5. During my absence from school, Manya also coordinated all class and homework assignments with George and my teachers.
6. Throughout life, my sister has done so many more things

for others and me. If I named them all, we probably would still be here next week. She should be an example for all of us."

Looking up, his voice cracked. "And there I thought she was so silly when she suggested to go to soccer practices with that gypsum mass on my foot and take notes. But she was right: as soon as my cast was off, I had no problems picking up.

"Before, during, and after my surgery, Manya never complained or showed a sign of weakness. She always motivated: 'Keep your chin up…you can do it…I believe in you…it's just a stepping-stone.'

"My sister has always been a loving, helpful, and positive person. I don't understand why she had to go." Sighing, the boy looked at his mother. "I miss Manya so much!" He rushed to his seat. Covering his eyes with his hands, Michael rested his head on his mother's shoulder.

"It's okay," Rosemary whispered. Gently stroking his upper arm, she kissed him on the temple.

Heiko stepped up. He introduced himself and placed a burgundy cloth bag on the pulpit. "Anke and I have known Manya for more than a decade. We had lots of fun at home, in school, and during our trips. Of all the years, the last one by far was the most eventful and the best. Manya, Anke, and I mastered our finals, made future plans for college and life, visited Mark without adult supervision for the very first time, and, most importantly, I proposed to Anke."

The teenager retrieved a framed photograph from the bag and showed it to the audience. "This is a picture of Anke and Manya posing like supermodels at a rest stop in the country during our last trip. It's the best image Manya could have ever left us with. Anke and I decided to always have an enlarged print in our future hallway."

He stowed the picture and pulled out two white papers. "Due to the unusual circumstances, I have asked for a partial advance of my inheritance. My parents granted my request and helped me purchase two early wedding gifts."

Heiko stared at his fiancée. "Since Anke was a little girl, she has always dreamed about owning horses. The photo I showed you minutes ago also has a black colt in the background. He and his mother gave us entertainment galore and have come up in many conversations since. In fact, Anke just mentioned them again last night."

He held up one sheet with his left hand. "This is the sales receipt for that particular colt and his mother. And this…" he said, raising his right hand with the other paper, "…is a contract to build a barn on our future property, starting next week. Boarding is paid for, and when my newlywed wife and I move into our home, the animals will move into their new stable as well."

Anke's tears of joy were followed by several sobs in the audience.

"I would like to leave you with a final thought," Heiko said and carefully placed the papers into the bag. "Even in time of hardships, life offers wonderful opportunities. We just have to figure out what those are and make them happen." Heiko walked back to his seat. Anke stopped crying and gratefully kissed him on the cheek.

Mark stepped up. "I decided to do something different and would like to express myself with a poem:

> Manya cheered me at any time and site.
> To know and to love her was my very delight.
> I wish I had told her my stance and my love.
> But now she's God's treasure in Heaven above.
> I can see her glowing angelic face.
> As she's smiling down from her permanent place.
> I am saddened that we had so soon depart.
> Forever I'll keep her locked in my heart.
> You never know what tomorrow will bring.

Make good decisions, live wisely, and
Give your best in everything."

Mark nodded at Manya's father and mother. "Mr. and Mrs. Mallwitz, I was privileged to have known your daughter. I'm so sorry for your loss." He stepped down.

Rosemary gave a short speech and invited attendees for a meal at the house after the burial. The pastor concluded the service. People expressed their condolences, picked up flower arrangements, and went outside. The chapel slowly emptied.

Regina hugged Manya's mother near the exit. "We'll see you in a bit. Take all the time you need." Rosemary nodded. Anke and Heiko followed Regina outside. Michael joined his father who gathered with Mark and two other men around the casket. Heinrich gave the cast and wreath to his son.

As Michael put his arm through the wreath, Anke's ribbon dropped down and formed a narrow tear-shaped loop. The boy discovered the engagement band on the bottom. Crossing looks with Mark, he asked, "Do you know anything about this?"

Mark shrugged his shoulders. "Anke insisted. Heiko approved. That's all there is."

"It's time," Rosemary said, waiting at the door. Heinrich, Mark, and the other men lifted the casket onto their shoulders and carried it outside. Michael and his mother followed.

A warm light breeze played with the ribbons and mourner's hair and clothing. Birds sang from the bushes. "Ging, gong. Ging, gong…" the bell loudly rang on top of the chapel, announcing the funeral.

Passing firs, bushes, evergreens, graves, people, and a cast-iron spigot, the pallbearers led the crowd to Manya's burial site. Meter-high rhododendrons, one yellow flowerbed, two strips of hoed soil, and a forty-centimeter unpaved path surrounded the tombstone and narrow deep grave.

After Michael placed the cast and wreath on top, the men lowered the coffin. People took turns paying their final respects;

staring, crying, whispering, speaking, praying, or by simply tossing single flowers into the grave.

Person after person left until only Mark, Rosemary, and Michael remained.

"Ready?" Mark asked.

Standing at the other end of the grave, Rosemary faced the back of her son. He stood in front of the headstone. She imagined him crying. Scratching her upper arm and looking up, Rosemary replied, "Better give us a few more minutes."

"I'll be waiting in the car," Mark said and walked away.

Michael knelt down and slowly glided his hand over the smooth black marble. He kissed the imprint and whispered, "I will never forget you." Rising, the boy wiped his knees. He turned and saw his mother staring at the grave. "Are you okay?" he asked and approached.

Without taking her eyes off the casket, she loudly breathed in and exhaled. "You know, I would have never imagined that one day I would be standing here, burying one of my children prematurely. This is not how life's supposed to be. I would have given anything, including my own life, to have her spared." She glanced at her son. "At least it's not as cold as yesterday or as stormy and rainy as the day before that. Manya couldn't have asked for more perfect weather."

"…And grandma couldn't have asked for better company," the boy said, staring at the second name on the gravestone: Erna L Mallwitz. He rested his head on his mother's shoulder.

A white dove flew on the tombstone. Cocking its head, the bird inspected the grieving humans. It strutted a few centimeters sideways, stopped, and cooed, "Grrrh, grrrh, grrrh…."

"Look, Mom," Michael whispered into his mother's ear. "A sign from Manya."

She said nothing and …cried.

As the dove flew off moments later, they walked away. Mark was still waiting. Michael and his mother got into his car. They drove off. Rosemary was glad to have a ride and that her friend Regina was already preparing the meal for the funeral guests at home. Good friends are truly priceless. Her thoughts drifted to Dieter Marro. He hadn't said much and only nodded when he left, right after they lowered Manya's casket. She wondered whether he went to work or to her house.

Arriving, Rosemary noticed the detective's car in front of her home. Accompanied by Mark and Michael, she went inside.

After the meal, the detective approached Rosemary in the hallway. Dishes clattered in the kitchen. People talked in the living room with the door open. "May I speak to you in private?" he asked.

"Sure," she replied, pointing at her bedroom. She wondered what he wanted. Several scenarios about her daughter's fate went through her head. "Are you okay? You've been very reserved today."

"I'm all right," Dieter Marro replied. "Just too many things going through my head." He went into her bedroom. She followed.

Three ivory wall units with matching nightstand, vanity, and double bed took most of the space. A square mirror and two angled rectangular side mirrors took the top half of the vanity. The bottom portion housed a wooden chair and several drawers on either side. Framed pictures of Manya and Michael hung on the walls and stood on the vanity amongst a bottle of perfume, lipstick, and a round flat tin of Florena hand lotion. The faint scent of vanilla hung in the air.

Offering him the vanity chair, she plopped herself on the quilt-covered bed. "What would you like to talk about?"

Sitting down, he lowered his voice. "Despite of what I've said in the past, I would like you to know something. However, as discussed, please keep the information confidential."

"You have my word."

"I meditated and meditated and decided to share this because I hope it'll be of some relief to you as it is to me." Trying to find the right words, he paused. "Manya left us with plenty of leads, which give me great confidence that I will solve her case soon and that justice will be served. Most importantly, I want you to know that your daughter's fate possibly also led us to a previous victim that otherwise might have never been discovered."

Shocked, Rosemary covered her mouth. Seeing herself in the vanity mirror, she placed her hand into her lap and stared at the detective.

Dieter Marro checked his watch and unexpectedly rose. "I better get going since I still have to finish some paperwork at the office." Rosemary followed him outside. "Keep in touch or call me if you need anything," he said.

She hugged him. "Thank you so much for sharing this… and thank you for the telephone. It's one of the best inventions ever."

"When did they install that?"

"This morning," she said, straightening her suit jacket. "But I've been so busy with the funeral, I haven't had a chance to tell you."

"That's okay. I'm glad you have it now. Just always remember…I'm only a phone call away."

She nodded and watched him take off.

23

"My goodness!" the lieutenant exclaimed, inspecting Dieter Marro's office from ceiling to floor. Stacks of cardboard boxes confined space to a six-meter cube and almost made him claustrophobic. White, white, everything was white except for the gray flooring.

"Tell me about it," the detective said, standing on a ladder and sliding a box with the code '1948-23' on top of another. His hands almost touched the ceiling.

"I wondered about your furniture in the hallway and never suspected anything like this. But now I know." Giving it some thought, his boss scratched his chin. "This room actually reminds me of The Great Wall of China."

Dieter Marro smiled. He stepped down and wiped his face. "I couldn't believe my eyes when the deliveryman kept coming back."

"How many did you get?"

"Three hundred forty-seven. I'll probably dream about boxes tonight."

"Could be worse like two thousand or so."

"I suppose," the detective said and spread his right fingers twice. "My hand is so sore and cramped up, it probably would fall off if I had that many."

Looking at several stacks, the lieutenant noted, "Nineteen forty-five, nineteen forty-six, nineteen forty-seven…I like your system; very clever."

"Best way to do it. However, I'd be lucky if I have a fourth reviewed by Christmas."

"It'll be only a matter of weeks, maybe even days. You'll see."

Dieter Marro wrinkled his forehead. "How would that be possible?"

"I made several arrangements."

"What kind of arrangements? More transfers?"

"Nope," the lieutenant said and grinned. "I rounded up three volunteers."

"Volunteers?"

"Yes. All men are retired, HR and board approved, and will be waiting for you tomorrow morning at the main entrance."

"How do you know them?"

"One of the guys, Gustav, went to school with me. He was a highway patrol officer for thirty-four years. Ever since the man took an early retirement, he's been helping human resources and administration twice a week."

"What's he doing for human resources and administration?"

His boss watched him start a new stack. "All sorts of stuff, including filing and mailing."

"Quite a change from working highways to an office job."

"He likes it. And, in case you're interested, he also plays rummy, bridge, and canasta."

"What about the other two?"

"They are Gus's friends."

"His canasta buddies?" The detective turned around. "You've got to be kidding."

Shaking his head, the lieutenant said, "Marro, you're on the wrong track. Just like Gus, his friends were decorated officers of the law. Friedrich worked in traffic and Kenny was a sheriff. Our captain and board members were impressed by their dedication and experience and gladly approved all men for the project. You couldn't ask for better volunteers."

Dieter Marro scratched his scalp. "How long do I get to keep 'em?"

"As long as it takes to get through all this," his boss said, pointing at several boxes, "weeks, months…they're open to any time frame."

"That's a relief," the detective said and pushed a box on top of another. Through the corner of his eye, he saw the lieutenant leave.

24

The entrance hall reminded Dieter Marro of a train station. People rushed back and forth. Some had uniforms. Others didn't. Many checked their watches and nodded at the guards, before disappearing behind different sets of tinted glass doors. A couple in their thirties gesticulated in front of an older security officer.

The detective approached the younger guard who had just hung up the phone. "I should have some people waiting for me?"

"All here," the security officer said and raised his eyebrows at the closest table in the waiting area. Tapping his left fingers on the mahogany security desk, Dieter Marro turned around. At the roped-off section, a blonde in her early forties talked to one of three gray-haired men. He recognized the woman from a few years ago. She used to work with his friend Ralf at the coroner's office before transferring to administration. The blonde left.

Dieter Marro turned to the security officer. "Do you have their badges?"

"Already distributed."

Approaching, he glanced from the president's picture in the waiting area to the visitors. "Good morning, gentlemen," he said. "I'm Superintendent Dieter Marro."

Introducing themselves, the men took turns shaking the detective's hand.

"Gustav Lehmann."

"Friedrich Beck."

"Kenny Meyers."

"If you'd please come with me," Dieter Marro said and entered the glass doors near the waiting area. A long hallway appeared. "So, Gustav, how long have you been playing cards?" the detective asked.

"Depends on what game you're talking about. I've played rummy for forty-nine and bridge and canasta for almost twenty-four years."

"Out of the three, which one is the easiest?"

"I'd say rummy is. I learned that game when I was nine." Wrinkling his forehead, he asked, "Why? Are you interested?"

"Perhaps."

Several officers and civilians walked by. Doors and lockers opened and closed.

"Quite a busy place," Friedrich Beck said and watched a K-9 unit approach. Gustav Lehmann gently elbowed his friend. "Never seen morning rush hour? I thought you worked in traffic." Both retirees chuckled.

Kenny Meyers gazed at his temporary badge. "Feels good to be important again." He deeply inhaled through his nose. "It even smells like my former work place here."

"Must be the old buildings," Dieter Marro said and led the men into his office. "This is it."

"Whoa!" Gustav Lehmann exclaimed as he walked in last. "What did I get myself into?"

"How many are there?" Friedrich Beck asked.

"Three hundred forty-seven," the detective replied.

Kenny Meyers whistled in amazement.

"It's been quite a challenge," Dieter Marro said and stretched his right hand. "All the writing, lifting, and stacking reminded me that I'm not in my teens anymore. I worked until midnight last night to get everything ready." Pointing at a stack of boxes with 1945-codes, he said, "We'll start over there and work our way through."

His boss's secretary entered through the open door. Carefully placing a tray with sugar, creamer, and four large cups on a short stack of boxes, she said, "Two coffees and two teas. Enjoy. I'll stop back in a couple of hours or so." She left.

Dieter Marro gave a short briefing. The men went to work.

Weeks and months of research went by. While the wall of cardboard boxes turned into a fortress of paper stacks, a small list of possible suspects evolved.

As the men studied files one rainy afternoon, Kenny Meyers suddenly said, "Wait a minute…I know this guy." The others looked up. He handed a photo to Dieter Marro and tapped his index finger on a man in the back row. "This is the one I'm talking about. Although, he looks way younger in this picture than when I met him."

"What's his name?" the detective asked.

"Arnold Behrens."

"Ar-nold-Beh-rens," Dieter Marro slowly repeated. "Well, the first name starts with an 'A' and…" he stared at the picture. "His features seem to match the Hof couple's description. That's good for a start. Would his character fit our profile?"

"Yes." Touching himself on the forehead, Kenny Meyers said, "Why didn't I think of him before?"

"When did he graduate?"

The former sheriff looked at the file. "Nineteen sixty-nine."

"How come you had to look it up? I thought you knew the guy."

"I do, but he was such a sore spot in my eye that I erased as much memory as possible."

"Besides the face and name, is there anything else you remember about him?"

"The man had a foul mouth, didn't care about others or himself, and had the most negative and aggressive attitude. He dragged everybody down, day in and day out, week after week. Would you like to have that kind of atmosphere on a regular basis?"

"No, not really."

"Why didn't they just fire him?" Gustav Lehmann inquired.

"Buddy, I discussed that with my superior many times but he didn't want anything to do with it. All I heard was that he wanted to give Arnold Behrens a chance to make something out of himself. So I went with it."

"What about the board?"

Kenny Meyers shrugged his shoulders. "Would you go over your captain's head right before retirement and take a chance of losing your job and some or all of your benefits?"

Gustav Lehmann shook his head.

"I didn't think so. But my dislike was based on several reasons and not just behavior or appearance. Right before I left, a rumor circled that the captain used to be close to Arnold Behrens's family."

"Close how?" Dieter Marro asked.

"Close in being the father's drinking buddy."

"Really?"

Kenny Meyers rubbed his nose. "Another rumor also stated that at Hartmut Behrens's deathbed Captain Clark promised to look after the son."

"I hate to ask: what was going on at your retirement?"

"Several people, including Arnold Behrens, applied for my position. However, one candidate after another mysteriously backed out until Arnold Behrens was the only one left. That man had no business or experience in becoming a sheriff."

"Do you think he blackmailed people?" Gustav Lehmann asked.

"Blackmailed or threatened them in some kind of way," Kenny Meyers replied and exhaled deeply. "In addition to several men, we also had a female applicant. Gossip made her a supermodel. Everybody wanted to catch a glimpse of her."

"What did she look like?" the detective inquired. The thought of another possible victim gave him goose bumps.

"Tall, slender, fair skin, blue eyes, and short blond hair; very pretty. The hiring officer told me it was her dream to become a sheriff. Believe it or not, she already had been a deputy for two years in another state."

Dieter Marro scratched his temple. "Why change the precinct with one foot in the door?"

"She moved to Lobau due to her husband's employment."

"I see."

"That woman should have taken my position," Kenny Meyers continued. "She had the knowledge, dream, and was a minority. Her backing out seemed very fishy to me."

"What do you mean by 'backing out?' Did she disappear or did she just withdraw her application? Elaborate."

"According to my friend from human resources, she withdrew her application and applied for something else."

"Did she at least get the other job?"

"Yes, but she only lasted for a year."

"When did you retire?"

"Three years ago," the former sheriff said.

"Ever seen Arnold Behrens's wife?"

Kenny Meyers widened his eyes. "That man had a wife? Why would anyone ever marry him?"

"I'll take that as a 'No.' Did he ever wear a wedding band or some sort of ring?"

"Not while I was around."

"Did I hear you mention Lobau?" Dieter Marro inquired. "Is that the police station you worked for?"

"Yes and yes."

The detective couldn't believe his luck. His feet tingled with excitement. "That's actually the precinct where my teenager's body was found." Exchanging looks with Kenny Meyers, he asked, "Could you stay a little longer today, so we can chat? Maybe something else will come to your mind."

"Sure, I'll stick around."

The special meeting with the retiree brought no new information. Three weeks later, all files had been reviewed. The list of suspects was tackled.

25

Dieter Marro and Kenny Meyers stepped into the small white building. Smoke hung in the air. Wrinkling his nose at his partner, the detective guessed 'Karo,' the only cigarette with this distinctive smell and strength. At the counter, a uniformed man talked to the only customer, a woman in a lilac knit dress. Beige filing cabinets divided the room in the back.

Dieter Marro signaled Kenny to follow and walked to the president's picture on the left. They studied the enlarged black-and-white photo. "How can people stand this?" the detective whispered. "The smell almost makes me nauseous."

"Nobody smoked when I was around," his partner replied with a low voice. He gave it some thought. "With all things said and done and current circumstances, I'm beginning to wonder if I ever should have retired. Maybe I could have even saved a life or two."

"No offense," the detective said, still whispering. "But I don't think you could have changed a darn thing,"

"Have a good day," the woman said overly loud, attracting Kenny Meyers and Dieter Marro's attention. She left the counter. Looking at the detective, she abruptly lifted her chin up and exited.

Oh no, Dieter Marro thought. She must have gotten the impression we were talking about her. He shrugged his shoulders at his partner. They approached the counter.

"Good morning. I'm Superintendent Dieter Marro and this is my partner, Kenny Meyers. We're with the Halle crime scene unit." The men showed their identifications.

"Deputy Peter Larsen," the officer behind the counter said. "How may I help you?"

"Is Captain Clark available?" the detective asked.

"I'm sorry. The captain went home with the stomach flu. Would you like me to dispatch Sheriff Behrens?"

"That won't be necessary."

The phone rang.

"Excuse me," the deputy said and picked up the phone. "Deputy Peter Larsen, how can I help you? … Your cat is in the tree? … You'll need to call the local fire department. … That is correct. … They'll have ladders. … Yes, they'll reach that high. … Good bye." He hung up and shook his head. "Some folks…I tell you. Gentlemen, where were we?"

"May we talk to you?"

"Sure. How long will this take?"

"About a half hour."

Peter Larsen turned around. "Annemarie?"

"Yes, deputy," a chipper female voice came from the back.

"Could you please cover for a half hour or so?"

"I sure can. Ouch." A drawer screeched. Steps neared.

A blonde in her early twenties came up front. She wore a green maternity dress with white embroidery around the collar. Gently rubbing her large belly, she said, "We'll be glad to help out."

"If a customer comes in, start the paperwork and tell 'em I'll be available soon. Only disturb us if it's an emergency, okay?"

She nodded.

"You're the best." Flipping part of the counter up, Peter Larsen created a passage. He turned to the visitors. "Come."

"When do you expect the sheriff back?" Dieter Marro asked, stepping behind the counter after Kenny.

The deputy checked his watch. "He left twenty minutes ago for his rounds…so in about an hour, I'd say. Why are you asking?"

"Arnold Behrens may not have any knowledge of our visit. Otherwise, the investigation might be jeopardized."

Peter Larsen gazed at his administrative assistant and pretended zipping his lips.

"It's safe with me," she assured. The woman unexpectedly covered her upper belly with her hands and leaned forward. She uttered through her teeth, "Quite active today. I think we've got us a soccer player."

"Do you need a break?" the deputy asked.

"I'll be fine," she replied and straightened her posture. "I'm tough. Just go on and do your thing."

"Tough all right. Knowing you, you'd probably go into labor and not tell anybody until the baby says 'Hello' to the world."

She grinned.

"Silly stuff aside, if Sheriff Behrens returns and I'm still in the meeting, let me know right away."

The administrative assistant coughed. "May I make a suggestion?"

"Sure," Peter Larsen replied.

"Notifying you without telling him anything might only raise his suspicion. How about me distracting Sheriff Behrens until the building has cleared and you returned up front?"

"Excellent idea! Let's make that our plan." He slowly shook his head. "I sure hope you return soon after having that baby. You're the only one that keeps me going around here."

"The year will go by faster than you think."

He rolled his eyes at her. "One thing is for sure: it'll seem like an eternity."

The deputy took the men to a narrow gray room with a table, three chairs, a sink, and a shelf holding two cups, a bag of coffee, packages of tea, and an immersion heater. "Welcome to our break room. If you exchanged the furniture with a bed and toilet, you'd think you were in a prison cell. Have a seat." Peter Larsen pointed at the full ashtray on the table. "Does either one of you smoke?"

The visitors shook their heads.

Moving the ashtray to the sink, the deputy stared at the cigarette butts. "I despise tobacco products. The smell, mess, health and environmental risks are just unacceptable, especially when people are pregnant," he glanced toward the reception area.

"The chemicals from Arnold Behrens's cigarettes and the stress from his behavior will one day cause us all to die of some kind of cancer…with 'Us' I mean people working here. All that man does is satisfy his own desires. His attitude and foul mouth suck. I'm tired of his filthy clothing. I'm tired of overflowing ashtrays. And I'm tired of not being able to open any windows to at least air out the building."

"All your windows are jammed?" Dieter Marro asked.

"No, we're able to open them, but the sheriff doesn't let us."

"Why?"

"Nobody knows," Peter Larsen replied. "Control, maybe."

"What about Captain Clark?"

"He's got his own little caboose in the back with all kinds of luxuries. Between you and me, he seems to take on a liking to the sheriff. So I only inquire about job-related issues now. In regards to the sheriff, I think he's got something wrong in his head. It stinks to work with him."

"I assume Arnold Behrens is the only one smoking around here?"

"Correct."

"Any visitors in the break room lately; relatives, friends, fellow officers, or outsiders?"

"Everyone is intimidated by the sheriff. The reception area is as far as people will go."

"Okay." The detective removed a plastic bag from his briefcase and held it toward the sink. "May I?"

"Feel free. Take it all."

Dieter Marro carefully dumped the ashtray contents. "This might be very helpful." Sealing and stowing the bag in his briefcase, he joined Kenny at the table.

"So, what can I do for you?" the deputy asked and sat across from Dieter Marro.

"We're conducting a murder investigation and would like to ask you a few questions."

"A murder in our precinct?"

"Yes."

"I'm surprised. I mean, no offense to anyone; but if we had a killer on the loose, shouldn't I know about it?"

"Do you remember the body parts found at the ash deposit site?"

"As long as I live, I will never forget that image," Peter Larsen replied and paused. "Is that why you're here? I thought it was a cold case."

"Who said that?"

"Arnold Behrens."

Moments of silence went by.

"How did the sheriff react when he saw the body parts?" Dieter Marro inquired.

"He remained unusually calm, showed no emotions, and barely even reacted when the K-9 assistant sniffed his shoes."

"The dog sniffed him?"

"Yes!" the deputy exclaimed.

"What came out of that?"

"Nothing. Arnold Behrens blamed the dog's attraction on the scent from his dogs at home. Even though the K-9 officer doubted that, he ignored the incident. Why are you asking all these questions? Do you think the sheriff might be connected to the murder?"

"Possibly."

"I'm sure glad that you're already using caution around that man," Kenny said. "It might have saved your life."

Dieter Marro informed the deputy about Manya Mallwitz's last stop at the bakery, the laboratory results, interviews with the angler president and the Hof couple, and the possibility of another victim.

Giving the lab results some thought, Peter Larsen said, "But a lot of people fish or have German shepherds around here."

"His police academy records meet our suspect's criteria, plus we have the eyewitness accounts."

"The police academy makes behavior analyses on their

students?" Peter Larsen shook his head. "No...."

"They don't," the retired sheriff said. "During research, I just happened to come across Arnold Behrens's file. I remembered working with him."

"What precinct did you work for, if I may ask?"

"Lobau."

The deputy pondered. "I thought your name sounded familiar. You are the former sheriff! Captain Clark praised you so many times, I lost track of it." He rose and extended his hand toward Kenny. "It's an honor to meet you, sir." The men shook hands. Peter Larsen's facial expression changed. "What's gonna happen if Arnold Behrens is involved? Will they close this station?"

"I'd refrain from such drastic assumptions," Dieter Marro said.

Clearing his throat, the retired sheriff exclaimed, "Ease up! You might have some positive changes coming your way."

"Oh, I don't know," Peter Larsen said. "Arnold Behrens is so slick and manipulative; everything is probably more in his favor than in mine. Look how far he's gotten already. Besides, I'm not sure if I want to be sheriff anymore. The best training I get is from our captain during the time Arnold Behrens is off or calls in sick. Captain Clark has taught me more in those few weeks than the sheriff during the last three years combined. Even if I was the best student in the world, how much can I possibly learn from on-and-off sessions? It takes years to become efficient. How am I supposed to protect and serve if I don't even know my job well enough?"

"I'm sorry that you didn't get the proper guidance and training you deserve," Kenny said. "But you should never give up. Wasn't it your dream to become sheriff some day?"

Nodding, the deputy said, "Ever since I played with plastic guns and holsters at the age of six."

"I hate to break the news: but if you walk away now, you automatically will make Arnold Behrens a winner, regardless if he's convicted or not. Do you want that?"

"Not really; but what choice do I have? Let's be honest."

Shaking his head, the retired sheriff said, "I've had some pretty rough times in my life but I never gave up." He pointed at the detective. "This man, here, lost his wife and daughter in a horrible plane crash. And as far as I know, he never gave up."

"Don't get me wrong," Dieter Marro said. "I wanted to give up and wished numerous times that I was on that plane. But with the help from family and friends I kept plucking away…one day at a time. My job became my life's mission."

"He's now one of the highest decorated detectives in the nation," Kenny said. "Please think twice before making a decision you might regret for the rest of your life. Just wait and see what happens."

Peter Larsen nodded. "All right."

"Back to Arnold Behrens…" Dieter Marro said. "Ever seen or heard about his wife?"

"No, I've never seen or heard anything about a spouse. If you asked me, his property hasn't had a woman's touch for decades. No female I know of would allow that much litter and filth."

The detective took some notes.

"Does Arnold Behrens still live in the forest?" the retired sheriff inquired.

"Yes, I pick him up and drop him off at the house every day."

Dieter Marro flipped the page in his notebook. "Were you ever inside his house?"

"Are you kidding me? Not in a million years would I dare setting my foot into that yard or house. Besides the litter, he's also got those gnarling German shepherds. They'll tear you to shreds. I've seen them do it to a baby rabbit one day."

"Then how do you pick the man up?"

"I honk twice and stay in the car."

"Did you ever notice anything suspicious on his property?"

Peter Larsen shook his head. "No, not that I remember."

"Would you mind getting last year's logbook?"

"Not at all," the deputy said and left. He returned within minutes. His face was red and sweaty. "I searched the filing cabinet from front to back and top to bottom: the logbook seemed to have vanished into thin air."

"Do you happen to know if Arnold Behrens worked June sixth of last year?"

"June sixth? He was off."

"Are you certain?" Dieter Marro asked. "You answered the question rather quickly."

"That day is a sore subject to me."

"How come?"

Remembering the day like yesterday, Peter Larsen said, "It was my sister's fortieth birthday. I rented the town's spacious film and theater hall, catered meals, hired a band, and even bought train and bus tickets for relatives to come to her surprise party. Even though the day was marked on the department's calendar and the request turned in months in advance, Sheriff Behrens still messed it up. He called in sick that morning. I even remember him chuckling as he hung up the phone. And you know what the worst thing was?"

The detective shrugged his shoulders.

"Arnold Behrens started a three-week vacation the very next day. Couldn't he have waited one more day?"

"Interesting," Dieter Marro said and scratched his chin. "Did the sheriff ever mention what he was planning during his vacation?"

"No."

"Did you ever see him during his time off?"

The deputy shook his head. "Nope."

Gazing at the clock above the door, the detective rose. Forty minutes had already gone by. "We better get going," he said. "Find that logbook. It could be substantial evidence."

"Annemarie and I will put the office upside down until we

find it." His face suddenly lit up. "I just remembered something: Arnold Behrens knew one of the men at the ash deposit site. I believe he held some kind of important position at GEL Manufacturing."

Dieter Marro raised his eyebrows. "You just might have given us a significant piece of the puzzle."

Showing the men out, Peter Larsen said, "Good luck. Perhaps we'll see each other again."

Kenny shook the deputy's hand. "May I ask you a personal question?"

"Sure."

"If you had the chance, would you give your life to save somebody else's?"

"I certainly would."

The retired sheriff gently patted Peter Larsen on the shoulder. "You're a man of good character. I would like to make you a deal."

"What kind of deal?"

"If and when Arnold Behrens is put away, and I'm sure he will be, I'll partner up and teach you everything you need to know as a sheriff."

Dropping his jaw, the deputy stared at the man across from him. "But you are...."

"A senior citizen? Retirement is not a death sentence; it's an asset. I'm more with my wife, children, and grandchildren; watch animals from the back porch; and also have plenty of time to improve the lives of others by lending a hand. Why would I pass up this once-in-a-lifetime opportunity?"

"But why me? We just met today."

"From what I've seen, you've got what it takes to become one of the best sheriffs." Looking at the other man's chest, Kenny bobbed his head and said, "I can see the medals, ropes, and pins on you already. And you bet that I'll be at the nomination to congratulate you."

Peter Larsen didn't say a word.

"Will you accept my offer?"

"Well…um…of course I will. Thank you, thank you so much!"

The retired sheriff shook the deputy's hand with a firmer grip. "I'm looking forward working with you."

"Me too," Peter Larsen said and smiled. He watched the men take off.

One month passed.

26

Dieter Marro and his partner waited at the empty counter. Although smoke-filled, the Lobau Police Station was eerily quiet. What if Arnold Behrens went berserk and killed his staff, the detective thought. Chills ran down his spine as he remembered the chipper pregnant assistant.

"Hello!" Kenny shouted toward the back.

"I apologize," a female voice answered nearby. "I didn't hear you come in." A woman in her late teens popped up behind the counter. Her red hair was tangled. Lightly wrinkled, a blue cotton dress wrapped her body from the neck down. Holding a pearl earring toward the men, she said, "I lost the back to one of my studs and was searching the floor. How may I help you?"

The officers introduced themselves.

"We need to speak with Arnold Behrens," Dieter Marro said. "Has he returned from his patrol rounds?"

"Yes, he has. I'll take you to him." Passing the break room, she led the men to a small office in the back. The door was open. Here, the smoke was the heaviest. A strange yellowish film covered the apparent former white walls.

Dieter Marro could only imagine what the filterless cigarette would do to someone's lungs. His eyes stung. My goodness, I'm not sure how long I can take this, he thought. Foul body odor entered his nose. Turning his head, he discovered a golden plaque on the closed door across the hallway. He read: Tobias Clark.

The assistant knocked. "Sheriff, I've got a couple of gentlemen here that would like to speak with you."

"Who is it?" Arnold Behrens asked harshly.

"I'll let them tell you," she said and walked away. The men stepped inside and showed their badges. Nothing was on the sheriff's desk, except for a full ashtray. Not one book stood on the shelf near the door. A scratched briefcase with a torn lock leaned against a discolored office chair in one corner.

"I'm Superintendent Dieter Marro and this is Kenny Meyers," the detective said. "We're with…"

"I thought you retired?" Arnold Behrens interrupted, extinguishing his cigarette in the ashtray.

"I did," Kenny said. "However, I temporarily got reinstated."

Arnold Behrens eyed the former sheriff. "If you came to replace me, forget it! You'll never succeed."

Kenny shook his head. "You haven't changed a bit; still rude, filthy, and corrupt. Just look at yourself!"

"We're all grown men here," Dieter Marro said, examining Arnold Behrens's stained uniform and greasy hair. "Let's converse with decency and respect. May we sit down?"

The sheriff lit another cigarette. After taking a long drag, he pointed at two chairs near the door with his right hand holding the glimmering tobacco item. Ash trickled on the desk. Ignoring the litter, he leisurely took another drag and blew the smoke toward the visitors. "Sure. What's this all about?"

Kenny closed the door. He and the detective sat down.

Clearing his throat, Dieter Marro moved his chair closer to the sheriff. He retrieved a large gray book from his briefcase and placed it on the desk. An oversized wooden ruler protruded in the middle section. The detective put his right hand on the cover and looked the sheriff into the eye. "Where were you on June sixth of last year?"

"Where did you get that?" Arnold Behrens asked, narrowing his eyes at the object on his desk.

"Please answer the question."

Sheriff Behrens scratched the back of his head. "I was at work, of course. Now, where did you get that damn logbook? That's property of the station, you know!"

"Watch your language and answer: Did you call in on June sixth of last year?"

"Why would I? I was scheduled to be off for three weeks

the very next day. And, in case you're wondering, my fishing vacation always starts on June seventh…has been for the past eleven years, not a day sooner or later. Check the logbooks!"

"All right," the detective said. "Do you go fishing by yourself?"

Arnold Behrens shook his head. "I always go with a buddy of mine."

"What's his name?"

"Ulrich Frankfurter."

"Where does he work?"

"GEL Manufacturing."

"What's his position?"

Sucking on the cigarette, the sheriff narrowed his cheeks. He blew the smoke at his desk. "Director of operations."

Dieter Marro opened the logbook and crosswise aligned the ruler over the left page. Tapping on the outlined entry, he said, "According to last year's records, Peter Larsen worked June sixth."

Arnold Behrens took a quick drag and put the cigarette out. "What are you supposedly working on? The last time I checked, all cases in this precinct were solved."

"We're working on the Manya Mallwitz case," the detective said, turning the logbook around and pushing it across the desk toward the sheriff.

"Manya Mallwitz? Never heard of her." Arnold Behrens stared at the line above the ruler and smirked. "Where is the deputy's name? Anybody can see that the writing is smudged beyond recognition. I worked. And if Larsen stated that he was here, then he's lying."

Dieter Marro pulled the book back and interlocked his fingers over it. "Are you sure you didn't call in sick?"

"I'm outdoors year-around and therefore rarely get ill. I doubt I called in. Between you and me, Peter Larsen has severe psychological problems. Just take a closer look at him. He's already on his third wife. I strongly suggest that you double-check everything he says or does."

"You know what?" the detective said and bit his upper lip. "Your excuses and attitude are unacceptable. I've got news for you: Kenny and I already talked to your fishing buddy. He stated that you two went fishing on June eighth because you cancelled the day before. What do you have to say about that?"

"If you already know the answers, why are you still bothering me with all these questions?"

"Because we wanted to hear your side of the story. Innocent until proven guilty, you know."

The sheriff rolled his eyes. "Regardless what you allege or believe, you've got nothing on me…absolutely nothing…zilch, nada, zip."

"Let me tell you what I think happened on June sixth. During the early morning hours you roamed the streets near your property for whatever reason; maybe one of your dogs got loose. At some point you discovered the stranded bicyclist. She might have had a flat tire, was lost, or who knows what. The young woman asked for help. But instead of assisting, you lured her into the forest and took her against her will. You locked her up in some kind of dungeon like the evil witch in Hansel and Gretel. When she refused to comply with your demands, you abused, tortured, and killed her. And…"

"Nothing but pure speculations," Arnold Behrens interrupted.

"I'm not finished!" Dieter Marro shouted, rising. Adrenaline rushed through his body. Curling his right hand into a fist, he so badly wanted to land it into the sheriff's face.

"Dieter," Kenny whispered.

Wiping his forehead, the detective sat down. He took a deep breath, exhaled, and said, "And when Ulrich Frankfurter talked about GEL filling up the deposit site, you saw the perfect opportunity to dump the body."

"You've got it all wrong and should pay more attention to Larsen," Arnold Behrens said. "He was aware of deposit site activities because I told him. Did you know that his first wife left him and his second spouse mysteriously died at twenty-two? That sounds very fishy to me. What if he actually did something to them? Besides, I'm a very busy man and wouldn't have had the time to do all the things you're accusing me of. In case Ulrich failed to tell you, I do a lot more than fish."

"Like what?" Dieter Marro inquired. "Staking out victims?"

"No, absolutely not! I work on the house, take my dogs for a walk, organize the barn, collect firewood, hunt pheasants, wild boars, and deer to stock up on meat for winter. And in case you don't know: German shepherds eat a lot of meat." The sheriff leisurely crossed his arms over his chest and leaned back. "Regardless, I have the right to do whatever I want on my property. What do you have to say about that?"

The detective's hands trembled with fury. His face turned white. "How in the world can you remain so calm? We're speaking of a capital crime here, not some coffee gossip!"

Arnold Behrens licked his lips.

Scratching his left ear, Dieter Marro said, "By the way, how do you explain the disappearance of your very own wife?"

"My wife? She ran off about twenty years ago. And as far as I'm concerned, she never existed."

"Are you sure twenty and not fifteen years have passed?"

"What are you getting at?"

"I believe that you did the same to your wife as you did to Manya Mallwitz and that neither one of them had any chance of ever getting away from you. The women were human beings. Do you even understand the word 'Human'?"

Arnold Behrens lit another cigarette and stared at the wall across from him.

Turning the logbook over, the detective said, "I've got something that might be of interest to you."

"What could you possibly have that would interest me?"

Dieter Marro opened the back cover and picked up three paper slips. "One speeding ticket, a seat belt violation, and one citation for running a red light. All are dated June sixth of last year. Guess whose signature is on the bottom?"

"Mine."

The detective shook his head.

Arnold Behrens turned red. His eyes widened. He rose and slammed his fist on the table, sending book and ashtray airborne. "It's all a farce! I'm done talking to you! I want you out!" He squished his cigarette in the ashtray and opened the door. "Luisa!"

Dieter Marro stowed the book and traffic violations in his briefcase. "I wish that...I'll save my breath."

The assistant popped up in the door. "Yes, Sheriff Behrens."

"Show our visitors out," Arnold Behrens said. "We're done here."

She signaled the detective and his partner to follow. At the front, the assistant checked her surroundings before removing a white stuffed envelope from the bottom drawer of the closest filing cabinet. Giving the object to the detective, she whispered, "Regards from the deputy."

Dieter Marro and his partner left.

Several blocks from the Lobau Police Station, the detective stopped at a red light. Kenny happily rubbed his hands. "Peter Larsen is such a blessing! I'm so anxious to deliver the cigarettes to the lab, get Arnold Behrens arrested, and start training my student. I wish we could somehow speed up the process."

"Acceleration would be nice," Dieter Marro said, staring at the traffic signal. "I just wish the samples hadn't been lost in the first place."

"Well, that's in the past now. Think ahead: we soon might all have a safer country." The light turned green. Sighing, the detective put the car into gear and took off.

Two weeks went by.

27

Ear-numbing sirens disturbed the peace in the forest as seven police cars went up the windy, mud-covered road. The deeper the officers drove the denser the surrounding trees and bushes became. A young buck jumped up and galloped away.

"How much longer?" Dieter Marro asked.

"Almost there," Kenny replied.

Staring at the following cars, the detective said, "Seems like an eternity." As he turned back, two pheasants flew across nearly hitting the windshield. "Whoa!" Dieter Marro shouted and ducked. The road straightened. Small red bricks paved the way to the residential home.

After passing several wooden posts with partial picket sections, Kenny drove through the open gate.

Animal feces, chewed bones, a bird cadaver, torn leather collars, chains, muddy feeding bowls, and maggot and fly-covered food scraps littered the barren ground. Deep car tracks led behind the house. The detective shook his head. "How can anyone live like this?"

Stopping in front of a flat brick home, his partner said, "I asked myself the same question years ago when I picked him up for work a few times. Now it looks even worse."

A German shepherd came from behind the house, frantically barking. Oil and mud covered the clumped fur. The rib cage and hip protruded. Just like Maria Hof had described, Dieter Marro thought. Amazing how things can still be the same after so many years. Some people will never learn.

Near the front door, the chain suddenly jerked the animal back. Falling on her rear, the dog gasped for air. The men stepped behind the cars.

Using a bullhorn, Dieter Marro said, "Arnold Behrens, we have a warrant for your arrest. Call off the dog and come out with your hands up."

Moments of silence passed.

The detective repeated his demands, adding, "This is our last warning!"

Again, no response....

Dieter Marro pointed his right index finger at the house. Drawing their weapons, the officers advanced. The German shepherd bared its teeth and, full-forced, leaped at the closest man. As the chain ripped, a shot echoed. The animal dropped. Blood seeped from the dog's mouth and ear, as it lay lifeless on its side. Everybody stopped and stared.

"Are you okay?" Dieter Marro asked the shooter.

The officer bobbed his head. "I'm...I'm a-a-all r-r-right."

"Just take a deep breath and calm down."

The man exhaled aloud. "Am I g-g-glad th-th-that I'm a b-b-better sh-sh-shooter than sp-sp-speaker under d-d-distress."

"I'm glad too," the detective said and patted the officer on the shoulder. He turned to Kenny. "Check on the K-9. They should've fixed the tire by now."

His partner nodded. Stepping aside, he exchanged some information on his walkie-talkie.

Dieter Marro moved his arms toward the residence. "Let's keep going gentlemen!"

A dozen officers swerved around the house while another twelve followed the detective to the front door. Kenny caught up. Focusing on his partner, Dieter Marro asked, "What's the status?"

"They're coming up the road as we speak."

Leaning against the brickwork, the detective carefully pushed on the handle. The door was locked. Two officers rammed the entryway with a heavy steel bar busting the wood into several pieces. A foul odor greeted. Nude magazines, candy wrappers, knit hats, socks, shoes, mouse cadaver and droppings, one jar of nails, one hammer, one coat, newspapers, cigarettes and ash were strewn all over the hallway floor. Discolored tapestry separated from the walls at several places. Dust-laden spider webs hung from the light fixture and ceiling like fabric fringes.

"My goodness!" Dieter Marro shouted and wrinkled his nose. Kenny shook his head. An officer near the door covered his mouth and mumbled, "What a stinky mess."

Short breathing and squeaky shoes approached from the outside.

The detective stared at the entryway with anticipation. The K-9 unit entered.

"About time you got here," Dieter Marro said.

Rolling his eyes, the K-9 officer replied, "Let's not talk about it." Keeping a short leash on his dog, he headed for the filled wardrobe rack to his right. He obtained a black trench coat and held it in front of the K-9 assistant. "Arko, search!" The dog sniffed the garment and barked once. While officers spread through the house, the K-9 assistant led his master, Dieter Marro and his partner, and four other men to a small room in the back.

Smoke filled the air. In the center, a disarrayed feather blanket covered a crooked tower of three twin mattresses. Bed sheets, stained socks, underwear, crumpled uniform shirts, and a tipped-over ashtray with cigarettes lay strewn on the floor. A small television on a mahogany stand showed a black-and-white subtitled Russian movie.

"That man should be ashamed of himself," Kenny said and held his nose shut. The K-9 assistant sniffed the clothes, bedding, and carpet. Pulling his master to the tobacco-stained draperies, he barked twice.

"Good boy," the K-9 officer praised, pushing the long curtains aside. The window was open. Arko put his front paws on the windowsill and barked repeatedly.

Lifting the edge of the blanket, Dieter Marro touched the sheet underneath. "Still warm...."

"He's got to be close," Kenny noted. Tilting his head back and moving his nostrils, he sniffed the air. "The smoke seems recent."

"Good boy," the detective said, patting his partner on the back. "I just couldn't resist."

Kenny grinned.

The K-9 officer rolled his eyes back. Holding the window open with his right shoulder, he turned to his dog and loosened the leash. "Let's get him!" Dog and master jumped outside.

"Are you up to this?" Kenny asked Dieter Marro.

"Have to be. Thank goodness this is only a one-story home." The detective leaped outside.

Jumping, Kenny grumbled, "I'm getting too old for this." He, Dieter Marro, and the four men followed the K-9 unit to a large brick barn.

A young officer approached the detective near the entrance. "There's no sign of Arnold Behrens or anything out of the ordinary. What do you want us to do?"

"Has Gunter's team completed their search?" Dieter Marro inquired.

"Yep; same luck as ours."

"Double the parameter. I'm positive there's something out here. Dig up disturbed dirt, climb trees, comb moss, check bird's nests, look under every piece of foreign debris…whatever it takes."

"Yes, sir," the officer replied. Staying behind, he talked to somebody on his walkie-talkie.

Kenny unexpectedly pointed at the middle section of a withered tree to his left. "Look at this!"

Shocked, Dieter Marro widened his eyes. He gagged.

A deformed head of a wild bore hung on a thick branch. The eyes were dried up. The skin was shriveled. Countless flies hovered over the neck area, forming a black blanket.

"Dieter, if I ever do stuff like this, just shoot me," Kenny said.

"Oh believe me, I will."

"I think I'm gonna go to a bar and have me an ice-cold beer when I get back."

Dieter Marro wrinkled his forehead. "You don't drink or go to bars."

"I know. But this is one of those occasions."

"I'll go with you. I can't wait to get out of here."

The detective and Kenny focused on the others at the entrance. Arko profusely barked. His nose almost touched the door. Dieter Marro stepped aside and activated his walkie-talkie. Shielding his mouth, he said, "Sylvio, Gunter…send four people from each of your teams to the barn."

"Understood."

"Yes, sir."

As the detective stashed his walkie-talkie away, two officers already arrived. All men drew their weapons and followed the K-9 unit inside.

A narrow partially dimmed window above the entrance shed little light, outlining large and small objects throughout the building. The K-9 officer stopped the dog and searched the wall to his right. Dieter Marro combed the area to his left and activated a switch. The barn was illuminated.

Rabbit, Deer, and wild boar skins, antlers of various sizes, and a preserved grown eel hung from a large wooden beam along the center of the barn. Rusty garden tools with and without handles leaned against the wall to the right. Moldy piles of hay, firewood, and a wood chopping block with an ax sat in a large pool of water to the left. Discolored bird feces freckled the concrete flooring. It smelled like sewage.

"This guy is getting weirder by the minute," the detective whispered to Kenny.

Lowering his voice, his partner asked, "You think?"

"I see use for rabbit and deer fur…but wild boar? What's he gonna do with that?"

Kenny shrugged his shoulders. "Make a brush to scratch his back or who knows what…." The thought of scratching delicate skin with those harsh bristles gave Dieter Marro goose bumps. He shivered.

Arko led the men toward the far end of the building. Somebody shouted. "Crud!"

Raising his pistol instantly, the detective stopped and turned around. He discovered the rest of the requested officers and lowered his weapon. A deerskin swung back and forth. Leaning backwards and defensively raising his hands, one of his men followed the close object with his eyes. Dieter Marro exhaled aloud and joined Kenny.

Arko sniffed a large workbench. After circling the object, the dog scratched the ground and barked twice.

"Good boy," the K-9 officer said and observed the items on the workbench. "Hmm, I only see a few rags, boards, and small tools…nothing out of the ordinary." He checked underneath. "And all I see here is a thin layer of light brown sawdust, about one meter."

Checking the wooden boards on top, the detective said, "These are uncut. Where in the world is that sawdust from… firewood, lumber, some small mammal cage?" He turned around. The firewood amongst the hay was dark and rotted. Tool handles, he thought. No. Searching some more, he was unable to find any other wood except for the overhead beams. None of those had any cuts.

"Sawdust will absorb about anything, including blood," Kenny noted.

Dieter Marro bent down. He noticed that there was at least a meter distance between the lowest shelf and the concrete flooring, enough room for a large person to roll. He signaled the others to come closer. "Let's move the workbench…on three; one-two-three." The officers picked up the object and set it aside.

A meter-by-meter square of sawdust appeared. Arko darted forward. His paws dug into the material, poking and scratching. However, only a few chips loosened. The layer of sawdust seemed fortified like fossilized resin.

"What is this?" the K-9 officer asked.

"Never seen anything like it," the detective replied.

Pulling the dog aside, the K-9 officer commanded, "Arko, out! Sit!"

Obeying, the animal pointed his ears and watched.

Dieter Marro knelt down and gently glided his palms over the surface. "Give me a hand, Kenny." His partner knelt across from him. "Do you feel a rim?" the detective asked.

"I do," Kenny replied. "Let's find some crowbars."

The men searched the barn. Finding a large toolbox behind the hay, they removed one chisel, three crowbars, two tire irons, and four flat steel bars.

On command, the officers pried the patch open.

Arko whined. "I know," his master said, patting the animal on the head. "Hold on tight; you'll have to wait for my signal."

The smell of bleach and mold tickled Dieter Marro's nose. He sneezed. Signing to stay back, he turned on his flashlight and observed the opening. A narrow wooden staircase led down to a small room with canned fruits and vegetables.

The detective shouted, "Arnold Behrens, we have a warrant for your arrest! Come out with your hands up!"

Nothing but silence came from below.

Dieter Marro repeated his demand, adding, "Give up now, or we will send down the K-9."

The detective waited a few moments and wondered if the man was really down there. As he raised his thumb at the K-9 unit, a faint clicking came from downstairs. Closing in, several officers turned on their flashlights and pointed them into the room below.

The K-9 officer unhooked his dog's leash. "Go and get him, boy!"

Snarling, Arko dashed downstairs. Several gunshots echoed. The K-9 assistant painfully howled and turned silent.

"My God!" the K-9 officer yelled, placing his hands on top of his hat. "That animal just shot my dog!"

Repeated clicking filled the cellar.

"His clip is empty!" Dieter Marro exclaimed. "Let's mo-o-o-o-ve!" He followed his fellow officers down the steps.

Somebody yelled, "Behind the staircase!" Pistols clicked.

Flashlights flickered.

Discovering Arnold Behrens crouching under the steps, the detective shouted, "Come out with your hands up!"

The sheriff didn't budge. Making a grim face, he yelled, "Don't you touch me! You have no cause for my arrest!"

Somebody turned on the light.

"I've got his gun," a nearby officer said.

Looking at Arnold Behrens, Dieter Marro shook his head. "Get him out of there."

Kenny and seven other men pulled the sheriff out. A jar of canned cherries shattered on the ground. After a short shuffling, grunting, and pushing match, the former sheriff was forced on his stomach. The officers pinned him by his arms, legs, and upper back.

Snapping a handcuff around Arnold Behrens's left wrist and pulling it toward the other arm, Kenny said, "This is what I miss the most about my job: putting guys like you away."

Dieter Marro watched his partner put the other cuff around the man's right wrist. "No cause for your arrest? I think you have no cause for your freedom. By the way, you are under arrest for the murder of Manya Mallwitz."

A whimper near the stairs attracted attention. The K-9 assistant lay on his right side and barely lifted his head up. His left ear was severed and hung loosely by a thread of flesh. Blood covered his head and tail. Staring, he pushed his left front paw toward his master.

The K-9 officer quickly approached. Kneeling, he leaned over his dog and whispered, "Shshsh." He bit his left fist. "Hang in there, buddy. I'll get you to a hospital." Putting his head down, Arko closed his eyes. His master picked him up. Rising, he turned to the sheriff. "Why did you have to shoot my dog? Unlike you, he has never killed anyone. He probably even has more feelings than you'll ever have!" The K-9 officer rushed upstairs.

Dieter Marro stared at the sheriff's bloodstained top. "Oh,

Arnold Behrens, I almost forgot: you are also under arrest for attempted murder on Officer Arko Von der Thorpe."

"The beast? You're kidding me."

"Do I look like I'm joking? Let me make myself clear: attempted murder on a police officer has most serious charges. And for your sake, I hope the animal survives."

A car took off with sirens.

The detective pulled on the sheriff's arms. "Get up!"

Arnold Behrens rose and smirked.

"What are you grinning about?" Dieter Marro asked with a stern look on his face. He so wanted to put his hands around the other man's neck and squeeze the living daylight out of him. But he knew better.

"You've got nothing on me," the sheriff said calmly. "I'm innocent. Captain Clark will testify to that."

"Captain Clark? I don't think he'll come to your rescue any time soon. He was briefed about everything. And, for your information, he actually co-signed all papers for your arrest."

"Bogus, bogus, everything's bogus. You're trying to set me up."

"Set you up?" the detective asked. "How about the belt? Is that bogus too?"

"What belt?"

"Records show that you ordered a new uniform belt right after last year's vacation."

Arnold Behrens rolled his eyes back. "So?"

"You just acquired a new belt six months prior to that. You know, as well as I do, that our belts are so durable that you probably could even pull a car with it. The point is that the belt should have lasted longer than a half a year."

"I tore it on the workbench. What does the belt have to do with my arrest anyway? Are you charging me with the murder of a belt too?"

Dieter Marro loudly exhaled. "I bet my life's savings that the belt you replaced matches the marks and fibers on our victim's neck. Just too bad that we currently are unable to test DNA...but it will be only a matter of time."

"Do you have the belt?"

"No, not yet...but I've got plenty of other evidence like scales, resin, and eyewitness accounts. By the way, your forest mainly consists of blue spruce, doesn't it?"

"Fir, spruce, evergreens...those types of trees are everywhere, including people's yards. I don't think you've got a clue about what you're saying or doing."

"Don't insult my intelligence!" Dieter Marro slowly shook his head. "Why am I even wasting my breath on you?" Wiping his forehead, the detective calmly said, "Over the years, I've attained a lot of friends and connections. I promise that I will personally make sure that every grain of sand on your property gets turned over. And I guarantee you that crime scene will find more evidence than you could ever bear."

"You don't have a..."

"Search warrant?" The detective pulled a white paper from his back pocket, unfolded it, and held it in front of Arnold Behrens. "What do you think this is? I meant to give it to you sooner but haven't had the chance. Don't forget to check the signatures on the bottom. This paper was co-signed as well." He stuffed the document into the sheriff's chest pocket. "Here, the paper will be my gift to you today...denying you this would be unbearable to me. Now, get upstairs!"

As Dieter Marro and his team arrived at the front yard, several police cars pulled up. The detective recognized a friend in the first vehicle. Through his walkie-talkie, he advised the other squad leaders to gather their men and prepare for take off. Putting the detainee into his car, he signaled two officers to remain with him. Dieter Marro turned to Kenny. "I've got you some reinforcement. Keep a close eye on him while I'm gone."

"Where are you going?" his partner asked.

"I need to exchange a few words with my friend Paul from crime scene."

"Okay."

The detective left. He returned twenty minutes later. After relieving one of the two officers, Dieter Marro got into the driver seat. He started the car, turned around, and gazed at Arnold Behrens. "Scared?"

"Why?"

"Because I made it my mission to put you away for good. And, believe it or not, I will succeed."

Arnold Behrens turned his head sideways and stared out of the window. "Screw you."

Saying nothing, the detective buckled up and took off. He turned on the siren. Five police cars followed him closely to the station.

28

"Damn' it!" Dieter Marro shouted, slamming the folder into the open briefcase on his desk. He sat down and buried his head into his palms.

The lieutenant walked in. "I assume you received the results from the freezer sample?"

"Yep."

His boss patted him on the shoulder. "You did your very best. She was long gone before Manya Mallwitz even came into the picture." He placed a stack of papers in front of Dieter Marro and tapped it twice with his fingertips. "Here, this will help you refocus."

Glancing at the bundle, the detective was somewhat relieved. It was only a third of the size of the angler list. "What is this?"

"A list of all courthouses in the country. Pay them a visit. I suggest you start with our state. If you find Arnold Behrens's marriage record, notify me immediately."

"O-kay," Dieter Marro said slowly, placing the paper stack on top of the folder with the lab results. He closed his briefcase, rose, and put his coat on. His phone rang. He picked it up. "Superintendent Dieter Marro, how may I help you?" ... His face lit up. "Well, hi Kenny! How are you? ... I'm doing okay. How's training with Deputy Larsen coming? ... I'm happy to hear things are going well down there." He sighed. "I just wish I could say the same about here. ... No, we've got a few more developments. But listen, I'm just getting ready to head out. Let me call you tonight when I get back, all right? ... I'll talk to you then. Bye." He hung up and grinned. "Good old Kenny checking up with me."

The lieutenant waited at the door. "One more thing...."

Dieter Marro's smile faded. He glanced at his boss with anticipation and expected the worst.

"I ordered search warrants for all GEL deposit sites. If we

didn't have a cause then, we do now."

"I wish we would have done that sooner. Why didn't we?"

The lieutenant swept some lint from his shoulders and stared at the man behind the desk. "Think of yourself as a judge. Would you grant a search warrant if there was no probable cause and every person in your state was accounted for? What about the sheriff's involvement and his friendship with Tobias Clark? Would that have changed your decision or made it easier?"

"But every person wasn't accounted for."

"We didn't know that for sure, did we? One eyewitness…so many years ago…no missing person…no probable cause. Marro, fact is fact. Past is past. Just drop it and move on."

Dieter Marro bit his upper lip. Rising, he closed and picked up his briefcase and joined his boss at the door. "All right."

The lieutenant checked his watch. "Come, I'll walk with you to the parking lot since I'm heading out as well."

"Sounds good."

29

The detective walked into the yellow mansion. He thought about his search for Arnold Behrens's wife. Weeks had passed. The paperwork at some of the courthouses was very disorganized and overwhelming. Some staff was rude. But his efforts finally paid off. He refocused.

An oversized picture of the president hung across from the entrance. Photos of children, colorful drawings, and one oil painting of two angels clinging onto each other decorated the rest of the walls. Somebody played mellow piano music down the hallway. Young girls laughed outside.

A blond boy, about kindergarten-age, stood near the reception desk. Crocodile tears ran down his cheeks. His lower lip protruded. A woman in her early twenties knelt in front of him and gently stroked his hair. Her flawless make up, blue eyes, and shoulder-length brown hair reminded Dieter Marro of a doll his sister used to have but never played with.

"Just be patient," the lady comforted. "Only a few more days and your new parents will pick you up. Let me see if I can find you a toy." She rose and walked to a neatly arranged row of white plastic bins.

The child stopped crying. He wiped his face with the back of his right hand and watched. "Here we are," the woman cheerfully announced, opening the container with a five on the lid. She removed a small yellow dump truck and held it up. "How about this?"

Instantaneously, the boy's eyes widened. He happily nodded. She gave him the toy and discovered the detective near the entrance. "Oh, I'm sorry. I didn't notice you come in." The woman quickly straightened her blue polka-dot dress. "What can I help you with?"

"I'm Detective Dieter Marro. I have an appointment with Mrs. Schulz at three."

"Yes, we've been expecting you. For security purposes, may

I see your identification?" The detective showed his badge. "Thank you," she said and gazed at the sitting child who now hummed the tune of a truck engine while dumping imaginary loads on the ground. The woman turned to Dieter Marro. "Could you excuse me for a moment?"

"Sure."

"Thomas," she said, leaning downward and gently rubbing the boy's left shoulder. "I will take you back to the concert now, okay?"

The child rose and picked up the truck. Holding the toy close to his heart, he asked, "May I keep it?"

"Yes, you may," she replied and smiled. The boy reached for her closest hand.

As she took the child down the hallway, a door opened. The music became louder. A young man came out. Smiling, he said, "You beat me. I was just gonna come down and check on him."

"He's doing fine. The truck will keep him calm for a while."

"Good. Thank you. I'm sure glad you know what you're doing." The man took the boy inside and closed the door.

Returning, she announced, "I'm back. Now to you...." She sat behind the desk, marked something on a paper, and checked her watch. Picking up the phone, she dialed a few numbers. "Mrs. Schulz, the detective is here to see you. Should I bring him in? ... Okay, I'll let him know." She hung up. "Mrs. Schulz will be right with you. Have a seat." The woman pointed at a wooden chair that stood between the desk and a tall filing cabinet.

Dieter Marro sat down and studied his surroundings. Animal, teddy bear, and flower stickers covered much of the peeling paint and rust from the cabinet. A small crochet or knit runner hung over the top. In addition to crooked rows, some of its loops were bigger than others. The detective wondered if one of the older girls made it. He cast his eyes on the receptionist. She read some kind of magazine and once in a while puckered her lips or wrapped her hair around her right index finger.

A lady in a red skirt suit came out of the room near the entrance. She was about his sister's age. The woman smiled and extended her hand toward the detective. "Good afternoon, I am Melanie Schulz, the orphanage director. Pleasure to meet you."

He rose and shook her hand. "Superintendent Dieter Marro." Her strong, rather masculine, perfume tickled his nose.

"Would you like some coffee or tea?" she asked.

"No, thank you, ma'am."

"Please," the woman said and showed him into her office. The glue-smeared paper mache piggybank on her desk reminded the detective of his kindergarten years. Photography of families and children hung on bright yellow walls. Leveling with a tall filing cabinet, one bookcase held scholastic, science, and children's literature. Vintage toys decorated several shelves.

He discovered a different setting on the shelf across from the director's desk. A framed picture towered over Berlin memorabilia and a brown teddy bear covered with black crust where the left ear used to be. Why would anybody want to keep that around, he thought.

She pointed at a red armchair, closed the door, and sat behind her desk. "How may I help you?"

"I have a few questions and would like to pick up the file on one of your orphans."

"All our records are confidential. Do you have a court order?"

"I do," the detective said, removing a folded paper from his briefcase and handing it to her.

Melanie Schulz unfolded the document. Reading, she placed one hand on her chest and wrinkled her forehead. "Ines? Ines Dahlmann?"

"Correct."

"I haven't seen her for over sixteen years. What's going on? Is she all right?"

Dieter Marro shrugged his shoulders. "I'm unable to share any information with you at this time."

"If you think she might be involved in something, you're looking at the wrong person."

"What do you mean?"

"Ines would never hurt a soul," the woman said and stared at her desk. "She cared about people and had great values. Children looked up to her. And boy, was she talented…in fact, one of her art pieces is hanging near the entrance."

"The Michaelangelo-style painting?"

"You got it. The angels are supposed to represent her and her baby brother. They were very close. The girl always said that she'll become an angel when she dies and that she was looking forward to reunite with her brother some day."

"Why was she here?"

"She lost her parents and her sibling in a house fire."

He remembered the one-eared teddy bear on the shelf and wondered if it was connected. "Was she ever adopted?"

Melanie Schulz shook her head. "Plagued by horrible nightmares and sudden anxiety attacks, the girl bounced between foster homes and orphanage. It took years of counseling to turn her around. But by that time she was a teenager and hardly anybody showed interest in her anymore." She shrugged her shoulders. "Nobody ever worked out."

"That's too bad."

"Before we go on, let me tell the receptionist to get Ines's file. It might take her a while." She glanced at her filing cabinet. "The system in the basement is way different than the one upstairs." Melanie Schulz left. She returned within a couple of minutes. "Now, where were we?"

"I realize that many years have passed but I must ask: do you by chance still have a personal item of hers?"

Nodding, the woman rose. "When Ines left, she wanted me to have her Wuschel. I'll get him for you." He watched her walk toward the shelf behind him. She whispered, "Looks like you'll be going to a different home for a while." Returning, she gave him the burned teddy and framed photograph. "I have two pictures at home. This one I always keep in my office for a couple of reasons. One: children from her time still stop by once in a while to chat. They cherish seeing her picture. You must know that due to a tight budget and running high cost of developing film, we were unable to take any pictures of children, with the exception of one file photo. And I'm sure if the children had the choice of one additional picture of one orphanage resident, they would've picked her."

Dieter Marro studied the color photograph. Wearing the same outfit as today, the orphanage director embraced a petite teenager under the Berlin television tower. He was stunned: Ines's brown hair and eyes reminded him of Manya Mallwitz. It dawned on him that Ines also had a younger brother. What a coincident, he thought. "With that tight budget, how did you manage the additional pictures?"

"I paid for them with my own money."

"I see."

"Now to reason number two," she said and loudly exhaled. "This picture is very special to me as well. It is from our last outing. After that, the postal carrier returned my letters as undeliverable."

"Did you say you hadn't seen her for over sixteen years?"

"Correct." The lady sighed and sat down. "I miss her. You know, Ines was like a daughter to me." Somebody knocked. Lightly raising her voice, the orphanage director said, "Please come in."

The receptionist entered, carrying a green filing folder in her left arm. "I've got the requested records. Is there anything else you'd like me to do?"

"Not at this time," Melanie Schulz replied. "Thank you, sweetie."

The receptionist placed the file in front of the orphanage director, glanced at the detective, and left.

Staring at the photograph, Dieter Marro said, "Pretty girl." He carefully put the teddy bear and picture into the side compartment of his briefcase.

"That she is," Melanie Schulz said and opened the filing folder on her desk. After gliding her right hand over the top page, she closed the file and pushed it toward the detective. "I'm kind of curious though; does your visit have anything to do with Ines's husband?"

"I'm not at liberty to discuss any details."

"You know, I've never approved of that guy and still have no idea of what she ever saw in him. Maybe Ines was looking for some kind of father figure. Maybe she felt under pressure due to the fact that she had to leave the orphanage at the rightful age of 18. But regardless, that man was unacceptable in so many ways."

"Did he ever hit her?"

"No, I didn't see any violence."

"How about unexplained bruising or some kind of other marks on her face, limbs, or body?"

Melanie Schulz shook her head. "No violence, no bruising, no marks…nothing. We are trained to look out for stuff like that. No…the man was careless and disrespectful. On the day of his wedding he wore a stained shirt, sneakers with missing shoelaces, and holy jeans that even exposed part of his underwear. Arnold Behrens should have been ashamed of himself. Why would anybody show up like that to a ceremony, especially his own?"

The detective shrugged his shoulders.

"When Ines introduced me in the courthouse, he didn't even say 'Hi' or shook my hand. Instead, he leisurely lit a cigarette. One of the administrators, who happened to walk by, noticed and told him that he could only smoke outside. Boy, did he have an attitude! He threw the cigarette on the ground, squished it into pieces, and simply walked off." She loudly exhaled. "I wish I could have stopped her from marrying him. But at eighteen, she was an adult and I didn't want to interfere with her life." Shaking her head, the orphanage director said, "This mess is all my fault. I should have never given in."

"Given into what, if I may ask?"

"As soon as she finished her counseling sessions at the orphanage, Ines looked at life from a different angle. She talked about the future, asked a lot of questions, and acted more mature and responsible than ever. Right after her seventeenth birthday, she requested time for herself.

"The grocery store where she was taught to become a saleswoman even guaranteed her a position for five years upon completion of her apprenticeship. She had only been there for eleven months. At that point, I figured she was able to handle many things on her own and gave her the freedom she wanted. But never did I suspect of her getting involved with somebody like that."

"Did she ever tell you how she met Arnold Behrens?"

"She didn't have to; Ines and I passed him numerous times walking around Devils Lake."

Raising his brows, the detective scratched his left cheek. "The lake near the orphanage?"

"Yes. The water, vegetation, and peace drew her like a magnet. It was her refuge from the past. After circling the lake, Ines and I always sat down at her favorite spot to meditate." The woman gave it some thought. "But I suppose he also could have approached her at the grocery store. We all need to eat to live."

"What was Arnold Behrens doing at the lake?"

"He was fishing."

"By himself?"

"Sometimes by himself, other times with another man."

Two young girls loudly argued over a toy outside. A woman interfered. Melanie Schulz closed her window. "I apologize."

"Children will be children," he said and gazed at the folder in front of him. "Ever exchange a word with either man?"

She shook her head. "The only encounter I ever had with both men was the brief introduction at the courthouse."

"His fishing buddy was at the wedding?"

"Yes."

The detective rubbed his neck. "Do you remember his name?"

Melanie Schulz momentarily paused. "The one thing I do remember is that his first name started with a 'U' like Uwe or Udo." She shrugged her shoulders. "I'm sorry, if I'm not of much help. It's been too long."

"Good enough. That concludes my visit." Dieter Marro stashed the girl's file into his briefcase and followed the orphanage director to the exit.

She firmly pressed the detective's hand. "I want you to know that Ines was well taken care off, from baby check ups to adolescent dental visits. Everything is documented and in chronological order. You should have no problems finding the information you're looking for. If you have any questions, call me or leave a message at the orphanage. And one more thing: when you locate Ines, could you please let me know? I'd like to see her."

"I'll take that into consideration."

"I so wish I had adopted her."

"How come you didn't?" the detective asked, noticing that there was no music coming from the end of the hallway.

"I was going through a rough life at that time. In addition of being an alcoholic, my husband also cheated on me. I contemplated divorce for several years. Let's be honest: would you put a child into that kind of atmosphere?"

He shook his head.

Opening the door, she observed the children on the playground.

Dieter Marro discovered the toddler from earlier. Moving the hinged bed on his truck, the child now dumped a load of grass and dirt. The detective imagined him humming and smiled.

A red ball rolled to the orphanage director's left foot. She bent down.

Approaching, a young girl in a pink dress cried, "Mine! Mine!"

"It's all yours," Melanie Schulz calmly said. Straightening

up, she backed off and raised her hands defensively.

The girl picked up the ball and held it tightly to her chest. "Mine." She strutted away.

"Thank you for your time," Dieter Marro said and shook the orphanage director's hand. "Please keep our conversation confidential; no word to anyone."

"Yes, of course."

He departed.

30

Dieter Marro walked through the glass doors. Staring at the close empty table in the waiting area, he remembered meeting the three rummy friends. His thoughts wandered to Kenny. How odd it was that he had worked for the Lobau Police Station. How odd it was that Kenny also had Arnold Behrens's file for review. With the former sheriff's help, Manya's case finally came to a close. He thought about himself and remembered his boss wanting to make him his replacement next year. Things were looking up. For once after his wife's and daughter's death, he felt satisfied.

The detective rested his eyes on a man in a gray suit looking at the president's picture. A receding hairline revealed several maroon spots on the visitor's head. He had seen one of those in the newspapers before…whose head was it on? He gave it some thought. Oh, yeah: the Russian president who was just elected last year, Mikhail Gorbachev. Ralf's comment popped up. Yep, coroners would have an easy job identifying either one of these men, he thought.

His looks crossed with the younger guard at the reception desk. The security officer raised his eyebrows and tilted his head toward the man with the gray suit. Dieter Marro nodded. Approaching the visitor, he said, "Good morning, you must be Ulrich Frankfurter."

"Yes, I am," the other man replied.

The detective extended his right hand. "I'm Superintendent Dieter Marro."

"Nice to finally meet you in person," Ulrich Frankfurter said and firmly shook the detective's hand.

"Thanks for coming down here so quickly."

"Any time. You were lucky by calling me at work yesterday afternoon. A day later and I would have been gone for several weeks. My wife and I are taking an overseas trip to visit her family. How long will this take?"

"Two hours maximum."

Glancing at his watch, the man in the suit said, "As long as I'm able to leave by eleven…got to change clothes and a plane to catch."

"Let's get you signed in."

The men walked to the security desk. Ulrich Frankfurter handed his identification to the guard and watched the people coming through the entrance. The security officer looked at the document and compared the visitor's face and build before checking a stack of papers. He made a quick phone call, wrote something down, and returned the document. "Good Day!"

"Please follow me," Dieter Marro said and led his visitor to the back. He checked with the lieutenant's secretary. "Room one still available?"

The woman nodded. "Reserved for you all morning."

"Excellent." The detective took Ulrich Frankfurter to a small room with four chairs and a table. "Have a seat. Would you like coffee or tea?"

"Coffee, please. Black."

Dieter Marro left. He returned with two large ceramic cups. The man in the suit sat in the chair closest to the door. He sure is in a hurry, the detective thought and set the cups on the table. Shutting the door, he asked, "Let's get straight to business: how long have you known Arnold Behrens?"

"For over eighteen years."

"How did you two meet?"

Grabbing the closest mug, Ulrich Frankfurter took a sip. "I like to go fishing, especially when I have fights with my wife or stress at work. The sport relaxes me. On that particular day, I had a very big fight with Daniela. We argued about something. Maybe money. Instead of taking time to put the gear into the trunk as usual, I just threw it on the backbench and sped off. I even remember my tires squealing. Little did I know that radar was set up.

"Between home and Devils Lake, the police stopped my car. The officer introduced himself as Arnold Behrens. He took my driver's license and registration, walked around my car, and peeked inside. I also remember him asking where I worked. So I told him." Ulrich Frankfurter paused. "Is that even a standard question for a traffic stop?"

Dieter Marro shook his head. "All officers on the street follow strict protocol, which prohibits the request of personal information."

"What about him looking at my car?"

"An officer on duty has that right at any time." The detective drank from his cup. "How much did he fine you?"

"Nothing. He returned the documents and started a conversation about fishing. I agreed to meet him at the lake the next day. Did I do something wrong?"

A phone went off in another room. It stopped ringing.

"No, you're fine," Dieter Marro said. "Besides fishing, what else do you do at Devils Lake?"

"We drink beer, talk a little, and watch people."

"How often do you get together?"

"A few times a month."

"How did you two get to know Ines Dahlmann?" The detective thought about the orphanage director's statement and was curious.

"She and another woman popped up one year. The two would always walk the lake before sitting on the shore across from us. When the girl started walking alone, Arnold insisted on meeting her. He said that he liked her very much but was shy around women. So I helped him. I stopped and involved her in a conversation one day, which he later joined. Next thing I know, the two were getting married." He stared at the gold band on his ring finger and looked up. "No offense, but why didn't you ask me all this when we talked on the phone several weeks ago?"

"At that time we were unaware of which role you were playing. I apologize for the inconvenience."

"No worry; I'm glad I could help," Ulrich Frankfurter said and finished his coffee.

"Quite a distance to go fishing in the Baltic Sea. Why not stay at the lake?"

"The Baltic Sea offers a wide array of fish and a whole different atmosphere than life on land. The flashing light towers, empty horizon, splashing waves, clean air, passing ships, fresh breezes, screeching seagulls, and movement of the boat make me forget all my troubles. I love it!"

"Do you take the train up there?"

Scratching his birthmark, the man in the suit said, "No, we always take my Volvo. It's nice to be at our own pace and to be able to stop and stock up on food and supplies whenever we feel like or need it."

"Any particular town you shop in?"

"Usually Rostock."

"I see," the detective said. It dawned on him that the man in the suit not only had a birthmark like the Russian president but also drove a car from the Soviet Union. "Now to your work… how long have you been at GEL Manufacturing?"

"Thirty-two years; I joined a month after the company started."

"And you've been the director of operations ever since?"

"Yes," Ulrich Frankfurter replied, checking his watch.

"How many buildings does GEL own?"

"Thirty-seven."

"Who's in charge of the keys?"

"I am."

"How are they stored?"

"In a glass case on the wall in my office."

"Access?"

"Only the owner and I have a key."

"Ever had problems with the lock on the glass case, missing keys, or difficult employees?"

Ulrich Frankfurter shook his head. "No…never."

"Crime Scene only received four keys. I know you have more than four ash deposit sites, especially after heating that many buildings for all those years. Shouldn't each site have its own lock just like your buildings?"

"Buildings and deposit sites are two different things. In addition to expensive, high-tech equipment, the buildings permanently house our supply, products, vehicles, auto repair shop, and employee, service, and financial records. Ash deposit sites, on the other hand, are short lived and of much lesser value. Once a site is filled, it's done for. Therefore, we only install new locks every decade to cut cost."

"Who decided that and when?"

"Management made that suggestion a year after the company started. The board approved."

"What about the equipment at deposit sites?"

"All vehicles have always been accounted for, and we've never experienced any break-ins."

"What about dumping?"

Ulrich Frankfurter scratched the back of his neck. "Dumping? I think people prefer accessible forest over our secured, lame piece of land."

"I assume the keys given to Crime Scene were from the glass case?"

"Correct."

"Are there by chance any others out there?"

"The owner has duplicates of all master keys and, starting tomorrow, the supervisors will have a key for their deposit sites as well."

Dieter Marro finished his drink. "How did the supervisors gain access in the past?"

"I always had to come out and unlock the gates."

"And at the end of the day you returned?"

"Yep," Ulrich Frankfurter said, crossing his arms over his chest.

"Who was in charge of everything during your absence?"

"The owner."

"May I see the current master key?"

"Certainly," Ulrich Frankfurter said, pulling a ring with a dozen keys from his back pocket and placing it on his left palm. He selected a large key and held it toward the detective. "Here it is."

Dieter Marro raised his right hand. "I don't need it…just wanted to see."

The man in the suit stashed the keys away.

"Looked like you have personal keys on there as well?"

"I do. It makes transitions between work and home way easier."

"How about the time you go fishing in the Baltic Sea? Same set?"

"Yes, the boat and storage keys are on there as well."

"Has your key ring ever gone missing or been damaged?"

Ulrich Frankfurter nodded. "I lost a few when I was younger. So I learned to clip the key ring to a belt loop. Now, wearing suits and going fishing, I revamped my strategy and put all my keys in the back pocket. Last year, however, my key ring caught somewhere on the boat…you see, when I drink, I get a little forgetful and careless. As I sobered up the next morning, I noticed the damaged key ring on one of my right belt loops. Thank goodness, the ADS was the only one missing."

"ADS?"

"Short for the ash deposit site key."

"Oh. Carry on."

"I called the owner of GEL right away. He said not to worry since the key was lost so far away. And nothing really was ever out of the ordinary, except for when they found the …" He gave it some thought. "Wait a minute…you don't think Arnold would have anything to do with the torso or missing ADS, do you?"

"I'm not at liberty to discuss details of my cases. Does the company keep track of all sites each master key covers?"

The man in the suit focused on his cup. "Yes."

"Who would have that information?"

"Bookkeeping."

"Ever experienced Arnold Behrens as irrational or out of control?"

"Out of control? No. Irrational? Yes, he's had his moments. But we all do from time to time. I wouldn't think anything of it."

"Did Ines Dahlmann ever act frightened toward you or Arnold Behrens?"

"No…never."

"Have you ever seen suspicious marks on the young woman?"

Ulrich Frankfurter shook his head. "Nope."

"How was the fishing going after the two got acquainted?"

"Arnold and I only met once every two weeks. But six months after the wedding, he insisted on going to a different lake. After the switch, we went back to our old frequency. Then, a few years later, Arnold was adamant about fishing in the Baltic Sea."

"Any idea what triggered the changes?"

The man in the suit shook his head.

Dieter Marro had his suspicion. "How many times did you see Ines Dahlmann after she and Arnold Behrens were married?"

"About three more times before we switched lakes."

"This concludes my interview," Dieter Marro said, rising.

Ulrich Frankfurter followed the detective to the door. "You know, Arnold told me that you stopped at his work and asked him all kinds of questions. He swears he is innocent. I admit the man is irrational, drinks, and curses, but that doesn't make him guilty of whatever you're trying to get him for."

"Like I said, I'm not at liberty to discuss my cases." Dieter Marro escorted the other man to the main hall and signed him out. Shaking Ulrich Frankfurter's hand, he said, "Thanks for taking the time to help us. Have a save flight and enjoy your vacation." He watched the man in the suit walk out.

31

The detective covered a big yawn as he walked down the hallway. Once in a while, he nodded at passing officers. A bad feeling crept up. As he entered his office, the detective discovered his boss in the brown armchair. Not again, Dieter Marro thought. What did they find now…Ines? A wave of anger flared up. The food in his stomach felt like sweltering coal. "Good afternoon, lieutenant," he greeted and slowly sat behind his desk.

"Excellent job on the interview with Ulrich Frankfurter this morning," his boss said.

"Uhm…thanks."

"So one little phone call made the big difference?"

"Yep, Peter Larsen's memory of the blue Volvo and its driver was beyond superb," the detective said and glanced over the paperwork on his desk. It was the way he had left it before lunch. He relaxed.

"Luckily our country has proper vehicle registrations and lucky for you too that the orphanage director remembered the 'U' in the first name of the fishing pal." A faint smirk brightened his boss's face. "You had to keep the best news last, didn't you?"

"You waited in my office to make fun of me or to talk about the latest update on my case?"

The lieutenant's grin faded. "I'll give you the latest update I know of: while you were leisurely slurping your favorite tea in Room one, I received a phone call."

Dieter Marro felt a chill run down his spine. His boss's sarcasm doubled the significance. Oh, no, he thought and buried his head between his palms. "Let me guess: they found Ines Dahlmann."

"Looks like it. The remains are expected to arrive by this evening."

"What's her condition?"

"Severed limbs and head…just like Manya Mallwitz.

However, decomposition only left us with bones this time."

"But Ines's blood type is the same as the freezer sample."

"Anybody can have AB. The dental records will have to have the final say-so."

Shaking his head, the detective said, "That poor orphanage girl had nothing going in her life from the beginning to the end; absolutely nothing. As if the fire wasn't severe enough already." He sighed and looked up. "Manya Mallwitz, Ines Dahlmann…I wonder how many more victims are out there?"

His boss shrugged his shoulders. "My guess is as good as yours."

"Is this case bothering you like it does me?"

"Of course it bothers me, especially since I've got two daughters of my own." The lieutenant slowly rose, straightened his uniform jacket, and approached. Patting him on the left shoulder, he said, "But that doesn't mean I have to get riled up and beat myself over the head. Chin up, Marro! You've got to think positive. Thanks to evidence, Arnold Behrens will be permanently off the streets and do no more harm to society."

"Do you really think that? We've never had a case like this. What if he escapes or gets out after ten years?"

The lieutenant walked to the door, stopped, and turned around. He confidently nodded at the detective. "I'm sure. I'll see you when the results are in."

"Okay."

His boss left.

32

The prison bell rang. Four men in gray uniforms marched down the yellow musty hallway. They passed a security gate and several steel doors with concealed windows. The tallest officer crosschecked a paper with the numbers above each cell to his right. "Twenty one…twenty two…should be coming up…twenty three; here it is."

The men stopped. Keys rattled in a distance. A far gate closed.

Shoving the paper into his back pocket, the tall officer said, "Ready?" His accompanying men bobbed their heads. "Let's get this over with." He retrieved two pairs of shackles from his belt and opened the heavy door. The hinges squeaked. Arnold Behrens sat on his bed and jumped up.

Staring at the prisoner, the tall officer said, "It's time. Please come with us."

Passing several gates and countless cells, the men escorted Arnold Behrens to the far end of the building. The prisoner's ankle restraints clanked with each step.

"Did the president receive my letter?" Arnold Behrens inquired. "Am I acquitted?"

Nobody replied.

Slowing down, the shackled man raised his voice. "I want to know if the president received my letter. Is that so hard to answer?"

"Aggravation is pointless," the tall officer said. "Your file is sealed, and we have orders to refrain from any conversation with you. Let's pick up the pace. We're on a tight schedule here."

"C'mon!" Rolling his eyes, Arnold Behrens shook his head. "This is unacceptable. I will complain to the prison board."

The men walked into a large room with a row of reflective windows and a colored picture of the president. In the center, an officer sat at a steel desk with two chairs. Rectangular narrow pins, various-shaped medals, and a braided silver rope decorated his flawless gray uniform. Leaning back and interlocking his fingers over his belly, he scrutinized the prisoner.

The tall officer cuffed Arnold Behrens to one of the chairs at the desk. "Have a seat." His accompanying men followed him to the door. Arm-by-arm, the officers formed a chain blocking the only exit.

"I'm Colonel Fritz Kramer," the man behind the desk said and sat up. Briefly tapping his fingers on a black folder, he looked the prisoner into the eye. "Let's not play games; we both know why you're here."

"What about my…"

"I'm in charge!" the colonel cut him off. Veins elevated around Fritz Kramer's temples. His face turned red. "You will speak when I ask you to, understood?"

The prisoner stared at Erich Honecker's picture. Colonel Kramer pulled a gray pen from his inner chest pocket and opened the file on his desk. "What should I put down as your final request?"

"Final request? I thought I would be released." Arnold Behrens wrinkled his forehead and pointed at the president's picture. "I sent an appeal to that guy a week after I got here." He counted fingers on his right hand. "Four weeks ago!"

The colonel's veins popped out even more. "Show some respect here. The judge found you guilty of murder. Why in the world should President Honecker pardon you?"

"Because I am innocent," Arnold Behrens replied, shaking his head. "This is so very wrong. I want my freedom! I'm a human being!"

"Human being? I've read your file. It speaks for itself."

"You read a folder of lies. The evidence was tampered with, especially the lab samples. Peter Larsen did it! He's the wacko that should've been arrested and prosecuted, not me!"

"As a former officer of the law, you are aware that police laboratories operate under strict guidelines, including the double-checking of all results. How can they possibly be falsified? The samples from the freezer, eyewitness accounts of animal and domestic abuse, replaced uniform belt and similar marks on one of the victims, missing ash deposit site key, and not to forget: type 0 inside one of the nuts from your chainsaw, matching Ms. Mallwitz's blood type! Everything points to you, and only you. And I'm sure, with more scientific research down the road, DNA will link you to these women as well."

Fritz Kramer crossed his arms over his chest. His veins leveled. "For your information, the president himself ordered your execution yesterday. Would you like to see the facsimile with his seal and signature?"

Turning away, the shackled man gazed at the concrete flooring. Sweat accumulated on his face.

"Enough," the colonel said. "What's your final request?"

"Go to hell!"

Fritz Kramer signaled the lined-up officers to approach and wrote something on the top page. Looking at the prisoner, he announced, "Arnold Behrens, you are guilty of murder and, upon president's orders, are hereby sentenced to death."

Tipping his chair, the condemned man jumped up. He spat into the colonel's face before the tall officer and his men were able to pull him back.

"Take him!" Fritz Kramer shouted, pulling a brown handkerchief from his chest pocket. He wiped his face as the men exited.

Via a freight elevator, the four officers took Arnold Behrens to the level below. Scents of mildew, gunpowder, and body odor hung in the air. The men passed a blond woman in black scrubs pushing an empty gurney. After several turns, they stopped at the end of the hallway where two women in camouflage guarded a steel door. Holding banana-clip-laden Kalashnikovs over the right shoulders, they set an eerie atmosphere. Motionless, the guards stepped aside and let officers and prisoner enter.

The woman with the gurney caught up. Retrieving a folded black sheet from the shelf below, she nodded at the armed brunettes and waited.

Shots rang out.

-The End-

Epilogue

Manya, her younger brother, and her mother were very close. Family, friends, students, and teachers respected the girl for her outstanding grades, dependability, and many other positive traits. She was a role model.

Months after her disappearance, the girl's dismembered body was found at an ash deposit site. The homicide was traced back to a sheriff. It is yet unknown how many women Arnold Behrens actually murdered.

Manya rests with her maternal grandmother. Rosemary visits the burial site on a regular basis. Due to family wishes, the girl's grave is unlisted.

Media outlets still inquire about the murder at the family's former residence.

All names, locations, and certain details have been changed to protect identities.

Order Form

Postal Orders: Giant Andre Publishing, 942 Creston Avenue, Suite 202, Des Moines, IA, 50315-1803, U.S.A.

[_] Yes, I would like to order one (1) copy of <u>Double Cover Up</u> for $19.95. Please enclose $4.95 for shipping & handling. Make check payable to Giant Andre Publishing.

Sales tax: Iowa residents please include 6 % sales tax.
Orders by check: please allow 2 to 3 weeks for processing and delivery. A handling fee of $20 will be assessed on all returned checks.

Shipping by air or overnight: U.S.: Include $9.95 for shipping and handling.

International orders: First Class please enclose $15.00 for shipping and handling. Priority with insurance $45.00.

Internet orders: Visit www.HannahTrebec@~~GiantAndrePublishing~~.com.

Name: _____

Address: _____

City: _____

Telephone: _____

Email: _____

Comments: